S0-ACA-157

EUROPE AGAINST DE GAULLE

Also by John Pinder
Britain and the Common Market

———————

SPONSORED BY FEDERAL TRUST FOR EDUCATION AND RESEARCH

EUROPE AGAINST
DE GAULLE

JOHN PINDER

FREDERICK A. PRAEGER, *PUBLISHER*
NEW YORK . LONDON

FREDERICK A. PRAEGER, *Publisher*
64 University Place, New York 3, N.Y., U.S.A.
49 Great Ormond Street, London, W.C.1, England

Published in the United States of America in 1963
by Frederick A. Praeger, Inc., Publisher

PRINTED IN GREAT BRITAIN

CONTENTS

PART III   TOWARDS A FEDERAL EUROPE

PART IV   TOWARDS WORLD ORDER

CONCLUSION

PREFACE

THE title of this book is imperative rather than indicative. I have tried to explain why Europe must be against de Gaulle and how it can be successfully so.

But the title is also indicative in two senses. The natural temper of modern Europe, sick of war, prosperous, sophisticated and sceptical, is opposed to de Gaulle's autocracy and chauvinism. Having experienced extreme nationalism and been poisoned by its bitter fruits, the peoples of Europe have realised, sooner than those of other continents, the need for a radical change in their relationship with each other. The European Community is the result. But there is a danger that de Gaulle, by inducing a relapse into the nationalist past, will wreck the Community before it is complete.

In Britain, which was uniquely successful in the age of European nationalism and which suffered less than its neighbours in the cataclysm of 1939–45, the need for such a radical change has been only half-understood. Britain has consequently not yet adjusted itself to its decline from the world's greatest power to a middle-sized nation among others in Europe. Much of our present malaise is due to this failure to find our proper role in the world; and this book argues that it is in the context of the international Community that we can do so.

The title is also indicative in so far as the word Europe has come to express a political idea totally opposed to de Gaulle's antique chauvinism: the idea of a Community of nations that are together evolving a new form of international government. Outstanding among the "Europeans" who represent this idea is Jean Monnet, whose name has been much used in this book. This might not be welcome to him, for he is so devoted to democratic and collective methods of working that he could almost be said to practise a cult of impersonality. But he cannot escape from the impression that he has made on a generation of people who want to build a new and better international system in Europe and later in the wider world. I only hope he will excuse one of them for using his name to epitomise it.

Collective methods of working are, indeed, a necessity in a field too big for one man to till, and I too have taken advantage of the knowledge and experience of many friends. I must in particular thank the Trustees of the Federal Trust for allowing this book to appear in their series; those who have read the book in draft and given invaluable advice, including John Bowyer, François Duchêne, David Howell, Richard Mayne, Roy Pryce, Michael Shanks and Stuart Whyte; the staff of the Federal Trust, particularly Eileen Usher and Brigitte Marsh, for producing with great speed from my manuscript a text that pleased the publisher; and the publisher for putting up with a lot. Needless to say, anything that is still wrong is not their fault.

JOHN PINDER
August 1963.

PART I

DE GAULLE AGAINST EUROPE

I

DE GAULLE AGAINST THE WEST

EXCLUSION from the European Community is a sore blow for Britain. The full consequences may not emerge for some years but, if the exclusion were permanent, it could inflict the severest wounds that this nation has endured for centuries.

Debate during the negotiations centred around the early effects of membership on the British economy. There was reason to suppose that it would have benefited, but this heated controversy was largely irrelevant. Membership of the Community is for good, and must therefore be judged by taking the long view.

Much of British industry wanted to join because of its need for a wider market. With the growth of automation and large-scale commercial organisation, this argument will become steadily stronger. It would eventually be impossible, relying on a home market the size of Britain's, to sustain many sectors of industry at all; and the tendency for one or two big firms to dominate the market would be greatly increased. Exclusion from the wider market means denial of a large part of industrial progress, and hence reduced prospects for prosperity and economic strength.

Although a generation might pass before their results were seen in sharp relief, these economic forces could damage Britain much sooner. Continental industries, based on their big market, would press continuously against British exports throughout the world, blighting the balance of payments and hence economic growth.

Political weakness follows eventually from economic weakness. But if separation from the Economic Community were to mean exclusion from political union in Europe, Britain's political influence would decline more sharply. A realisation that power in the modern world could be retained only as part of a large, cohesive group was the basic motive for the British application to join. If Europe coalesces politically without

I

Britain, she will become a spectator on the touchline of world politics. Nor will the position be better if the Continent fails to unite, for Continental impotence would be matched by instability.

Sadder even than the loss of prosperity and power would be Britain's insulation from the experience of creating a Community of diverse nations. The crucial political and moral problem of this age is to get the nations to live together in peace. The European Community has gone farther than any other institution in limiting the power of its member-nations to do each other harm. Outside it, the British people will be unable to contribute much to solving this predominant problem.

At the same time as de Gaulle's axe fell on Britain's application to join the Community, he also struck at the Community itself and at the idea of a partnership between Europe and America. He had always been hostile to the new European institutions and, as Head of the French State, had usually referred to them in terms of denigration. But hitherto his opposition had been cautiously obstructive. In casting his veto on Britain, however, he blatantly ignored the Community method of arriving at common decisions by patient discussion within the Brussels institutions and by the composition of national wills. Instead, without reference to anybody, he made his will clear at a press conference and imposed it by *diktat* in Brussels: this, moreover, in regard to the most important question that had faced the Economic Community in its five years of existence. Not only has much of the mutual trust on which the Community experiment was based been lost; there is a deep fear that the next time de Gaulle's will differs from that of France's partners—which is far from unlikely to happen —he will destroy this product of so many years of patient work to build a better political system in Europe.

Just as de Gaulle's dislike of the Community method has been ill-concealed, so has his hostility to America. The Community Europeans, on the contrary, have been staunch upholders of the Atlantic alliance and of economic collaboration with the United States. The doctrine of partnership had been evolved to consolidate this co-operation. But the anti-American tone of de Gaulle's press conference and his rude refusal to discuss defence co-operation with America made it clear that he was likely to try to sabotage this idea as well.

It is no coincidence that de Gaulle has struck at Britain's interests, the Community method and Atlantic partnership at one and the same time. The motive for all three acts of aggression was the same : his one political passion : to increase the power of the French State. Britain in the European Community would have rivalled France for its leadership; therefore, unless there was any compelling reason to the contrary, Britain should be kept out. The Community itself, with its highly organised institutions, was designed to remove part of the process of taking decisions, in matters of common concern, from Paris to Brussels; therefore the Community's wings should be clipped. America's crime was to be much stronger than France; so American influence should be ejected from Europe, which would be reorganised under French hegemony.

This passion for national power sets de Gaulle against the postwar tidal movement towards the coalescence of the West. He has a special grudge against institutions that include America or Britain, for France cannot be top nation in them. But even on the Continent of Europe, where France could, at least for a time, be the leader of the Six, he bitterly opposes the methods of working together that have been evolved by Jean Monnet and other great Europeans and embodied in the European Communities. For whereas these institutions are based on the search for common interests and the will to common action, de Gaulle's thinking begins and ends with the interests, which mean for him the power, of France. These two lines of thought may converge for a time, as was shown by de Gaulle's tolerance of the Communities for four years in order to retain the alliance of the Five, but the conceptions are so fundamentally different that de Gaulle is almost bound to oppose any further application of Monnet's ideas of international democracy whether in Europe or on a wider scale.

Even if de Gaulle does no more than obstruct the development of Community and partnership for a few years he will do great harm. For there is an urgent need for more organisation and government at the international level. Without it there is grave danger that the history of the 'thirties will be repeated : that international institutions will be too feeble, in a world economy that is developing serious weaknesses, to provide stability and a framework for growth; and that a mixture of narrow nationalism and blind complacency will undermine security and endanger peace.

Thus de Gaulle's veto is not just a blow at Britain, although it is indeed a bad one. He has at the same time created a crisis for Europe and the West. For his assault on the process of Community and partnership weakens the means whereby the West can help to solve the terrible problems of the age and thus makes it more likely that the world will either collapse into anarchy or fall subject to communist domination.

It is against this background that the veto on Britain must be viewed. To see it, as de Gaulle undoubtedly does, as just another round in the age-old series of conflicts between England and France is useless. Britain might well lose, as France is in a strong position inside the Community and Britain is an outsider. But in reality nobody would win a struggle on nationalist lines; for Europe would be sliding down the Gadarene slope of nationalist rivalry and antagonism, when the interests of all its peoples can be served only by the strengthening of international order and government.

The struggle must be seen, then, not as a duel between England and France but as a conflict between chauvinism and the methods of international democracy that were being evolved in the European Community; and the first task is for Europe to overcome or by-pass gaullism and make progress again in developing the Community idea.

The European Community, which is the foundation for Atlantic partnership and contains the seeds of a world order, cannot be built without either Britain or France. One or the other is needed as a counterweight to Germany and to provide a reservoir of diplomatic experience and skill. Britain's absence has not mattered so much in the past because France was there, leading in the Community's construction. But now that France is at best a weak link and at worst a hostile force, Britain's aloofness from the Community idea has become not only damaging to herself but also a menace to the whole structure. This book is an endeavour to show what Britain can do to help restore the momentum of Community Europe; what are the prospects and the right policies for the "Europeans" on the Continent; and how America can lend its support : in short, what the West must do in order to repulse de Gaulle and to resume its progress towards a completed European Community, an Atlantic partnership and a better-organised, more just and peaceful world.

MONNET'S EUROPE ·

In the short space of thirty years Europe suffered the agony and carnage of the First World War, the long misery of the Great Depression, the lunatic nationalism of the Nazis and the unbelievable horrors of the Second World War. Almost the whole world was sucked into the vortex of these terrible events. People on the Continent of Europe, however, had felt the fullest impact, and they emerged in 1945 determined that Europe at least should never again be responsible for such disasters.

The conviction grew that the root of the evil had been the unchecked sovereignty of nation-states. If the nations were to join together in setting up a common government, war between them could be prevented, the problems that lead to war resolved and economic difficulties caused by national frontiers surmounted.

It was not long before these opinions crystallised into a strong movement for the federation of Europe. In France, Germany, Italy and the Benelux countries the great bulk of the democratic political forces, in particular the Socialists, Christian Democrats and Liberals, were in sympathy. This "classe politique" was inspired and brilliantly led by Jean Monnet and quite a small number of dedicated federalists.

In Britain and other European countries, few of which had felt during the war the same shock to their social and political life as the Six, this movement was weak. Nor did most of the nations in other continents wish to change the existing international system based on the nation-state. America and Russia were powerful enough to play the leading parts within that system; and the emergent peoples who had won their sovereignty were fiercely determined not to dilute it.

It was therefore in the Six that Monnet's ideas took root and began to grow. Their essence was to apply the federal principle of international democracy to solve current political problems, in a way that took full account of political realities. This practical approach flourished and the result was the three European Communities.

Because the ideas were essentially practical, however, and because Monnet and his friends were empiricists who believed in solving concrete problems rather than inventing titles and constitutions, the words that have been developed to describe this process and its promoters and supporters are strangely inadequate. The latter have often been called the Europeans. But this is ambiguous : does it refer to supporters of the European Community, or to all the inhabitants of Europe? The "federalists" or the "European Movement" are too narrow; each is identified with organisations that do not embody all the support for the European Community and to which Monnet himself does not belong. The "good Europeans" sounds too pious; most of these men are after all statesmen and politicians, not saints. The "Europeans" in quotation marks is clearer, but they cannot stay in their quotation marks for ever. *Faute de mieux*, they are called in this book the Europeans without quotation marks, and the reader will have to remember that the word refers to the promoters and supporters of the Community idea, rather than to the people of Europe at large.

Nor are we better provided with words to describe the kind of Europe that these Europeans have been constructing. Little Europe is a ludicrous misnomer for a region containing more people than the United States. Community Europe or the European Community focuses too much on the economic Communities in their present form. Without the addition of a Political and a Defence Community; without the reform of the Community structure so as to eliminate the national veto and strengthen the European Parliament's control; and without political systems in the member-countries that ensure a humane and democratic body politic with a liberal view of the world, the European Community is not the Europe that the Europeans have envisaged. Federal Europe gives a better indication of the end, although it can be misleading to fix attention on the political structure of old federations like the United States; nor does "federal Europe" give any hint of the empirical process of integration that has been developed, or of the political outlook of the Europeans and their view of Europe's place in the world. Instead of these terms, therefore, this book coins the name "Monnet's Europe" to denote the

Europe that the Europeans have been building and against which de Gaulle has now thrown down his gauntlet.

There is a danger that, by thus identifying the new Europe with the name of Jean Monnet, the impression will be given that it is the work of one man who is something of a dictator. Nothing could be further from the truth. The essence of Monnet's method is democratic and collective. Whether as the head of the French Commissariat au Plan, of the High Authority of the European Coal and Steel Community, or of the Action Committee for the United States of Europe, he has always worked by involving many people in the making of policies and the taking of decisions. He has therefore driven in harness with men such as Spaak, Schuman, de Gasperi, Adenauer, Hallstein and Mansholt, who have played a major part in building the new Europe, as well as with hundreds of others less famous. Monnet is, indeed, so free from any cult of personality that the use of his name implies, paradoxically, a Europe conceived in terms not of personalities but of ideas and institutions.

Aims: pacific, democratic, liberal

The first aim of the Europeans was to put an end to war between European states. If it has become hard to imagine that such a war could ever again break out, this is largely thanks to the Europeans' work. Before they had embodied common interests in the Community structure and thus reduced traditional sources of conflict such as the Saar to relative insignificance, the peace of Western Europe could not be taken for granted at all; and the establishment of that peace to the exclusion of all possibility of another European war was the first objective of Monnet's Europe.

Thus, a lasting peace between France and Germany was the explicit purpose of the Schuman Plan to establish the European Coal and Steel Community. "The solidarity in production thus established will make it plain that any war between France and Germany becomes not merely unthinkable, but materially impossible" was how M. Schuman himself put it.[1] And after a year as President of ECSC Monnet said: "Today peace depends not only on treaties or promises. It

[1] From a statement made by Robert Schuman, French Foreign Minister, in announcing the proposal for a Coal and Steel Community, 9 May 1950.

depends essentially on the creation of conditions which, if they do not change the nature of men, at least guide their behaviour towards each other in a peaceful direction. That is one of the essential consequences of the transformation of Europe which is the object of our Community... Faire l'Europe, c'est faire la paix."[1]

The Europeans, then, were seeking a way to remove from their countries the power to make war against each other. Often in history a period of stability has been secured by means of empire or hegemony. But the Europeans were determined not to allow any one nation to dominate the others. With the wounds of Nazi oppression still raw, they insisted on creating a system of international democracy in which each nation would carry its due weight and no single member would outweigh the rest. As Monnet said recently : "We have had and have as our objective essentially the creation of a United Europe and the elimination between nations and their peoples of the spirit of domination that has brought the world close to destruction many times."[2] And following de Gaulle's veto on British entry into the Common Market, Professor Hallstein affirmed that "the Community system, the constitution of the Community, is of itself a negation of any hegemony, the organised and methodical rebuttal of hegemony".[3]

It would not be consistent to put an end to the domination of one nation over the others within Europe, only to allow the European nations as a whole to fall under the sway of an outside power. There was a deep fear, after the Russian armies had rolled forward to the Elbe, that if the West were divided and weak the Russians would extend their primitive and brutal political system over the whole of Europe. This was a pressing motive for Western unity and the American alliance.

Had resistance to the expansion of Soviet communism been the only aim, however, the Europeans could have been satisfied with Western unity in the form of the American giant leading and protecting a number of West European dwarfs. This has, indeed, been the pattern since the war and, although not explicitly stated and perhaps not even clearly understood in these terms, the essence of British policy seems to have been

[1] Speech by Jean Monnet at Aachen, 17 May 1953.
[2] Address by Jean Monnet in New York, 23 January 1963.
[3] Statement made to the European Parliament by Professor Dr. Walter Hallstein, 5 February 1963.

to preserve it. The Europeans, on the other hand, while keenly aware of their common interests with America and of the need for the Atlantic alliance, and recognising that American predominance is essential while Europe is weak, have wanted to avoid being subject to an American hegemony for ever. The doctrine of the two pillars of the alliance has therefore been evolved: a European Political Community, with institutions to ensure that its members acted together, would have weight enough to become an equal partner with the United States. The American government for its part, being genuinely anti-imperialist and not wishing to exercise a hegemony over its allies, also supports this doctrine.

In some British minds, the idea of the two pillars has become confused with gaullism or neutralism. But these things are quite different. De Gaulle attacks the Atlantic alliance because he wants the French armed forces, complete with H-bombs, to act independently of, and perhaps in opposition to, the United States. Neutralists want Europe to contract out of all alliances and become a big Sweden. Most Europeans, on the contrary, want to make the alliance with America still closer, while reducing as far as possible Europe's inferior status within it.

This point is of the utmost importance because, while few would begrudge the Europeans the Community's internal peace and prosperity, many in Britain, particularly on the Left, have accused them of fomenting a new European nationalism that could do great harm to the world at large. Among all those people in the Six who have supported the establishment of the Communities there is certainly a spectrum of opinions, ranging from a gaullist to a neutralist attitude towards the outside world. But the attitude of Monnet and the majority of the Europeans is liberal: they want to develop good relations between Europe and other continents. They do not believe, however, that good relations will be improved if Europe degenerates, through lack of unity, into a modern Balkans, without the power to exert much influence over its own fate. Monnet himself, indeed, goes further and sees the Community method of curbing national power as a process that will spread until it is used not only between close associates such as Europe and America but also to solve the great world problems of disarmament and economic development. This "spillover process", which may be called Monnet's revolution, is considered in more detail in the next chapter.

Because the Europeans' first successes have been in the economic field, these political aims—peace and democracy in Europe and the restoration of Europe's influence in the world—have been pushed into the background by the economic objectives. The Europeans believed that their national economic frontiers were shutting the people of Europe out from the prosperity and productive power that the Americans had achieved; and they hoped, by abolishing those frontiers, to reap the benefits of large-scale production for a vast continental market. This was certainly a most important aim, and the influence of the Common Market on Europe's prosperity, and of that prosperity on the improved political stability of postwar Europe, should not be underestimated. But even in the economic field, much of the Community's steam has been generated by the desire to rectify the injustices between one man and another that are caused by the existence of national frontiers between them; and this essentially political motive, of eliminating the distortions imposed by national frontiers on the relations between a man and his neighbour, has always been predominant.

Thus the purpose of Monnet's Europe may be summarised as a decisive break with the chauvinistic nationalism of the past. This does not imply an undervaluation of the European nations, which are, and will for generations remain, the stuff of European society and politics. But the Europeans have rejected the theory that the nation-state is an all-embracing entity, the only duty of whose citizens is to be its servants. Hitler's insanities and the excesses of fascism embodied this creed at its most virulent; and it is widely realised that de Gaulle and Beaverbrook suffer from a milder form of the disease. What is not so commonly understood is that a refusal to accept the idea of supranational institutions, an insistence on the nation-state as the only source of political authority, is in fact an essential part of the theory; and that Britain's policies in Europe since the war have contained a strong element of this.

There have always been prophets who understood that relations between man and man of whatever nation were more important than a man's links with his state. But now that modern transport and communications have brought the nations close together, this kinship with men across the frontiers is much more widely sensed. Thus, whereas in the past only

prophets looked forward to an order in which common citizenship would be shared by many nations, enough people now
accept this idea, at least in Europe, to make it the basis of a
political reality. This is the essential aim of Monnet's Europe,
most succinctly expressed by Monnet himself: "Nous ne
coalisons pas des états, nous unissons des hommes."[1]

Methods: federal, pragmatic

The problem for the Europeans was, then, to find a political
method that would enable a form of common citizenship to
replace the old system of national absolutism. The Community
type of organisation, embodied in the three European Communities that have been established, is their solution.

The fundamental principle of the Communities, which
distinguishes them from international organisations established
in the past, is that the governments of member-states no
longer insist on their own interpretation of their national
interest as the ultima ratio, before which all other interests
must give way. They have agreed to institutions which ensure
that, in certain matters, the general interest will prevail over
a particular national interest. The Court of Justice, European
Parliament and independent European Commission all play
their part in this, but the very centre of the whole conception
is the provision for many important decisions to be taken by
majority vote.

Thus in the Economic Community, majority voting is
being introduced for tariffs and import quotas, and for policies
on agriculture, transport, and monopolies and cartels. International organisations established in the past, such as the
League of Nations, the United Nations, the OEEC or NATO,
have been based on the opposite principle of the unanimous
vote on essential matters, giving each member a veto with
which to impose his will, or rather his won't. This follows
inevitably from the doctrine that the national government is
the ultimate political reality: the nation's veto is the symbol
of its absolute sovereignty.

Common sense indicates that if everybody has to agree before anything is decided, there are not likely to be many
decisions, and those that are taken will be the lowest common
denominator of opinions. The only group that is known to

[1] Speech by Jean Monnet to the National Press Club, Washington, 30
April 1952.

work effectively with a system of unanimity is the Quakers, who feel themselves under a moral compulsion to reach agreement. But national governments are not like Quakers. They go to international meetings in order to protect their national interests; and there is often one or more with a positive desire to prevent agreement from being reached at all.

In these circumstances, it is not surprising that experience shows coalitions or international organisations based on the unanimity principle to be at best unwieldy and at worst totally ineffectual. Thus Mr. Kennan has written, after many years of acutely intelligent observation of international relations: "One sees the almost insoluble technical problem that is inherent in coalition diplomacy as such. This is aside from the question of differences of outlook in themselves. It is the problem of how such differences are to be reconciled in such a manner as to permit a flexible, alert, and firm conduct of policy on behalf of the group as a whole. An occasional single decision is by no means enough."[1] Kennan is writing about a coalition's attempts to conduct a joint foreign policy, where the need for quick reactions is often greater than when a group of nations is considering the group's internal affairs; but the problems of a coalition in forming policies about such "internal" affairs are not much less. As Kennan says: "Coalitions find it possible to agree, as a rule, only on what not to do. This is why their tendency is so often to do nothing at all."[2]

Where one nation is much stronger than the rest, like the United States in NATO and Britain in the early years of OEEC, such international bodies or coalitions can be made to work. But they do not work well; the weaker partners are usually discontented; and, as these examples show, when the weaker partners increase their strength the system becomes increasingly strained.

Having decided that national governments and national interests were no longer the be-all and end-all of politics, then, the Europeans concluded that the new system should be based on the majority vote. The veto as the symbol of national sovereignty would be replaced, at the heart of the Community institutions, by the majority vote, as both the symbol that the general interest is more important than any particular

[1] George F. Kennan, *Russia and the West under Lenin and Stalin*, Hutchinson, London 1961, p. 147.　　　[2] *Ibid.* p. 45.

national interest, and the practical mechanism for translating the general interest into effective decisions.

Thus the Europeans bravely grasped the nettle of sovereignty. But they applied the federal principle of the majority vote in a most pragmatic way, taking full account of political realities and national susceptibilities.

In the first place, the system was applied only to solve pressing problems for which any lesser solution was clearly undesirable. Thus the Europeans' first great success was the establishment of the European Coal and Steel Community, designed to contain a revived German steel industry. The post-war policy of preventing its revival had been shown to be economic nonsense : Western Germany, like Britain, must import food and raw materials in order to live, and it could not pay its way without a steel industry as the basis for its exports of engineering products. But an independent national steel industry in Germany evoked intolerable memories of ruthless cartels and the arsenals of war, and the only alternatives were a German industry subjected to international control or a European framework strong enough to hold it. The allies did not intend to subject Germany indefinitely to a semi-colonial status, so a strong European framework was the only acceptable solution. Although the British government was not willing to help in working out this solution, the French Foreign Minister, Robert Schuman, instigated by Jean Monnet, proposed a supranational body within which neither Germany nor any other member could unilaterally control its own industry, and the Coal and Steel Community was established.

Similar pragmatic reasons underlay the choice of the majority vote for two of the most important subjects in the Economic Community : the external tariff and agricultural policy. The Six, for valid economic and political reasons, wanted to merge their six national markets into a single common market. They believed that a free trade area, with widely differing national tariff barriers towards the outside world, would be hard to work. But if a common tariff could be changed only by a unanimous vote, the Common Market would be an impossibly unwieldy unit in international tariff negotiations; the low-tariff countries in particular—Germany and Benelux—feared that no tariff cut would ever get past the veto of a protectionist member-government. It was therefore necessary to provide for changing the common tariff by

majority vote if the Common Market was to be established.
Likewise for agriculture the majority system was essential. The
Common Market was not attractive to France, Italy or Holland unless trade was freed in agriculture as well as industrial
products. But national agricultural policies are so complex that
a detailed scheme for fair and free trade in agriculture could
not be worked out before the Rome Treaty was completed.
So it was essential for France and the other agricultural exporters that Germany, the main importer, should not be able
to veto proposals for freeing agricultural trade within the
Common Market; and it was agreed that agricultural policies
would eventually be decided by majority vote.

Thus the principle of the majority vote was not applied to
any important subject without strong practical reasons, which
made both unilateral action and a veto on common decisions
unacceptable. Where possible, too, common action was laid
down in advance in precise and detailed agreements, so that
governments would know exactly to what they were committed. This method was used for the central feature of the
Common Market: the internal disarmament of tariffs and
quotas and the erection of the common outer tariff. In this
essential matter, then, the governments did not sign a blank
cheque but knew their obligations in advance. This had the
further advantage that the main provisions of the Treaty—
what has been described as its backbone—would proceed
automatically, without the checks and setbacks that are in-
evitable if decisions have to be taken *ambulando*; and this
generates a political momentum that enables decisions on
other questions to be taken more easily.

The national governments' fears of the majority vote were
also calmed by the use of qualified majorities. Formally this
was a two-thirds majority in the Community's system of
weighted votes: four each for France, Germany and Italy,
two each for Belgium and Holland and one for Luxembourg.
In practice, while excluding any national veto, it allowed one
of the big three to prevent a decision if it had the support of
Belgium or Holland, and it prevented the small three from
being over-ridden by the big three unless the latter were supported by the independent European Commission. Thus a
majority would be hard, but not impossible, to get against
the opposition of a big member or of the small Benelux members acting together.

It will be noticed that the big three, France, Germany and Italy, have equal voting power that corresponds to their roughly equal size. This balance of weight between the larger members is itself an essential part of the Community method. If one member were big enough to dominate the rest, the Community would be no more than a highly organised and effective hegemony, just as the German Empire was in reality a takeover of the other German states by Prussia, which had nearly a third of the votes in its Council and the bulk of its military power. But as Monnet and Hallstein have so forcibly stated, the Community was designed to prevent any such hegemony or domination. For this reason it was impossible to conceive a Community consisting only of Germany, Italy and Benelux; for Italy, despite its large population, has been and still is economically weak in relation to Germany, which would therefore dominate such a Community. This was unacceptable not just because of the recent experience of wartime domination by Germany, although that was clearly a factor; there was no room, in the democratic structure that the Europeans were determined to build, for the Community to be dominated by any one people. In these circumstances, Britain and France were the only countries that could provide a counterweight to Germany. But Britain was not interested in taking part. French participation was therefore essential to the whole venture. This largely explains the strength of the French bargaining position within the Six and the inability of the other Five to progress with Monnet's Europe, whether by means of the European Defence Community, a Political Community, or a strengthening of the European Parliament or of other aspects of the Economic Community, when the French government does not agree.

The invention of the independent European Commission was another safeguard against the domination of a minority by a majority line-up. In addition to its responsibility for executing Community decisions, the Commission has to make the proposals on which those decisions are based. The Council of Ministers, in which the national governments are represented, cannot take decisions by majority or qualified majority except on proposals put to it by the Commission. It must either accept the Commission's proposal, or reject it and ask the Commission to try again, or amend it unanimously—in which case there is, of course, no possibility of a minority's being over-ruled. The Commission, whose members are charged with finding solutions that are in the general interest, and are forbidden to take orders from national governments, is not likely to prepare policies that would consistently harm any one member and benefit the rest. Thus the powers of the Commission which, with the Parliament and Court of Justice, represents the more federal aspect of the institutions, have been cleverly combined with those of the Council, representing the national interests, to serve as another protection against abuse of the majority system.

Then again, in order further to allay national fears and to avoid the hasty use of a majority vote before the institutions had been run in and the members were accustomed to working smoothly together, the idea of the transitional period was used. Decisions on agriculture and the common tariff, for example, must be made unanimously until the third stage, which is due to begin on 1 January 1966. Thereafter the qualified majority applies.

Even where a majority vote has been allowed under one of the Community Treaties, the Six have taken great pains to give full consideration to any minority view. The majority has spent much time and care in trying to understand the needs of the minority; and the minority has felt obliged to seek a compromise.

In all these ways the working of the majority system was softened and made as painless as possible for any national government that might find itself in the minority. But it was nevertheless in the background, inducing a climate in which clear decisions would be taken. M. Etienne Hirsch, formerly President of Euratom, has put it as follows: "Most of the decisions [in the Euratom and Common Market Councils] are unanimous. This makes it easy to underestimate the importance of the stipulations for majority voting. Nothing is more of an illusion, for only the possibility of a majority decision . . . makes possible mutual concessions and reciprocal adjustments. On the other hand, the unanimity which overlies the right of veto makes such adjustments impossible, and leads either to an alignment based on the least positive position, or to paralysis pure and simple."[1] Without the possibility of a majority vote, the whole institutional apparatus of Parliament,

[1] European Parliament, *Débats*, No. 50, 20 December 1961, p. 124.

Court and Commission would be of little use. Built around the majority principle, the apparatus works.

Thus the Communities are the product of a pragmatic federalism. They embody all possible adaptations to reality and concessions to nationalism, but the federal principle of the majority vote, with the institutional implications of parliament, executive and court, is there. The Europeans have tended to avoid using the word "federal" because it evokes strong passions. Many people, especially in Britain, have claimed that it implies subjection to a blueprint that regulates the smallest details in advance. The word "communautaire" has therefore been coined to describe the Community method.

But most of those who dislike the word federal are not in fact objecting to the regulation of details in advance. If they were, they would find the extremely detailed blueprint for internal tariff disarmament the most objectionable feature of the Rome Treaty. This, however, is hardly ever criticised; indeed, it would have been adopted by anti-federalist governments as part of the scheme for a general European Free Trade Area. The objectors' target has really been the principle of transferring any authority from national governments to common institutions in which decisions would be taken by nations acting together, however much influence the governments were to have in these institutions and whatever safeguards were provided against the abuse of the majority system.

The Europeans have made great progress by means of the "soft sell": minimising the radical nature of the changes they proposed. But in the long run this cannot and should not be minimised. De Gaulle for one has understood the intensely political nature of what the Europeans are trying to do: political in the sense of changing the structure of power: who decides what, where and by what procedures. So has Beaverbrook. And both of them pull out all the stops of nationalist sentiment in opposing any such change: de Gaulle by insisting that the functions of the Brussels institutions are purely technical; the Beaverbrook press by plain abuse directed at any such institutions.

It is therefore no longer useful to try to avoid evoking strong passions. Strong passions have already been evoked. It is now necessary to project as clearly as possible the changes that are proposed and the reasons why they are proposed, and this cannot be done by avoiding the best words available, even if they cause opposition. Monnet has rightly said that the "procedure for collective decisions is something quite new and, as far as I know, has no analogy in any traditional system . . . . . there is no central government; the nations take their decisions together in the Council of Ministers".[1] But the five dots represent the words "It is not federal because", which cannot be so readily accepted. For the central feature of the Community is that the seat of power to decide on certain matters of vital common concern is being transferred from the several national governments to a common institution in which the national governments collectively, and acting by majority vote, have the main power of decision. The essence of the case for the Community is that the seat of power needs to be transferred in this way; the word federal seems the best to describe the process; and the word federal should therefore be used.

Weaknesses: incompleteness, concessions to nationalism

Indeed, the chief defect of the Community institutions is not that they are too federal but that they are too pragmatic; that, in their pragmatism, the Europeans have made, or had to make, too many concessions to the nationalists. Thus it may be contended that all the means described above of drawing the teeth of the majority vote have left it without enough bite to do its job; and that the qualified majority might more appropriately be called the qualified veto. Only time can prove whether this is true. In the next year or two, for example, it will be seen whether the delay until 1966 in the application of majority voting for agriculture and the common tariff is going to wreck the prospects for Western trade co-operation; and other tests will follow later on. In the meanwhile, it cannot be denied that it was necessary to weaken the majority principle if national governments were to agree to set the institutions up at all; and probably desirable in order to secure the continued collaboration of the national political and administrative machines.

What is more disturbing about the existing Communities is their incompleteness. When a single market is established, it follows that common economic and financial policies are required to guide and regulate it. Yet decisions on such poli-

[1] Address by Jean Monnet at the Second World Congress of Man-made Fibres, London, 1 May 1962.

cies can be made only by unanimity. No great strains had resulted up to the middle of 1963, with the internal tariffs cut by no more than half and with prevailing conditions of boom; but when the tariffs have been cut more deeply, and if there is recession instead of boom, the effect of divergent national policies may be very damaging. Even under the most favourable conditions, the slight revaluation of the German mark caused some complaints. The troubles in the stagnant coal industry have indicated the difficulties when times are not so good. A unilateral devaluation of a major currency by, say, twenty per cent during a recession could strain the Community so much that it would fall apart; and if there are not to be such devaluations, recovery must be ensured by common economic policies.

Another serious blemish in the Communities is the relative strength of the Council of Ministers and weakness of the European Parliament. The Parliament's only real power is the right to dismiss the European Commission by a two-thirds majority. But if this deterrent is the only weapon it is not likely to be used; when hanging was the only penalty prescribed by law for sheep-stealing, juries were reluctant to convict. Apart from this right of dismissal, the Parliament has to rely on persuasion, to which the Commission is generally sensitive but the Council of Ministers not.

The concentration of power in the Council of Ministers is not so undemocratic as some people make out. The Ministers are after all the representatives of duly constituted governments, responsible (though now only formally so in France) to their respective national parliaments. And this criticism comes ill from such British people as have insisted that in international bodies all power should rest in the hands of national governments, thus reducing the Assembly of the Council of Europe, for example, to impotence. But the democratic structure of the Communities would be strengthened by giving the European Parliament more power to legislate, control the budget and make executive appointments; and this strengthening of the Parliament is especially desirable when democratic control through the Council of Ministers is sapped by the weakening of democracy in France.

Finally, the Communities have responsibilities only in the economic field and not in the other main sectors of common concern to their members: foreign policy and defence. There is a strong possibility of conflict between the external commercial policy of the Community, which will be decided by majority vote, and the other aspects of foreign policy which are still decided by the national governments acting separately; and the physical basis of power—the armed forces—rests entirely with the national governments, which can therefore in the last analysis defy the Community or break it up. Indeed, the fundamental aim of the Europeans, to replace the use of power politics and the possibility of war between members by a civilised political system and the rule of law, will not have been securely and finally achieved so long as the members dispose of their separate national armed forces.

It is not fair to accuse the Europeans of ignoring these limitations. When the Americans rightly insisted on the rearmament of Germany, the Europeans proposed the European Defence Community as a means of integrating German armed forces securely into a European framework, just as the German steel industry had been integrated into the ECSC. But although the EDC was accepted by France's five partners, it was wrecked on the twin rocks of British indifference and French nationalism. If the British had participated the French would have agreed, but those Frenchmen who were afraid of EDC without British participation were joined by the communists and by those, such as the gaullists, who were against it because they could not bear to see the French Army integrated into a European Army, and the French Assembly voted the proposal down. Thus a direct assault on the citadel of national sovereignty through the integration of the armed forces was repulsed and the Europeans had to return to the economic trail blazed first by the ECSC and later turned into a beaten track by the EEC and Euratom.

As will be seen, these weaknesses of the Community—the absolute or qualified vetoes, the weak system for forming common economic and financial policies, and the omission of foreign policy and defence from the scope of the Community method—leave it open to obstruction or sabotage by a truculent member-government. It depends for its working on mutual trust and, to some extent, on members behaving as if it were already a federation although it is not: using the Community institutions to the full and avoiding the use of naked national power. This is especially true during the first two stages of the transitional period, when the veto still

applies to the most important questions. Fortunately, up to the
end of 1962, this mutual trust existed. The Communities were
in their honeymoon period and this, with the momentum
generated by the backbone of the scheduled changes in tariffs,
carried them forward on a wave of great success.

Results: prosperity, political progress

By 1962 the Europeans, using these Community methods,
had made progress towards achieving their aims to an extent
that would have been unbelievable ten years earlier.

The economic success of the Common Market had been
astounding. Between 1958 and 1962, tariffs between the members had been cut in half; trade between them had almost
doubled. While the Common Market is by no means the only
cause of its members' unprecedented prosperity, it has contributed to the remarkable prolongation of the postwar boom
and of exceptionally fast growth rates on the Continent, more
because the idea of an economic federation has caught the
imaginations of industrialists and broadened their horizons
than because of the actual effect of the tariff cuts on prices
and through prices on trade.

The Community had also contributed to social progress.
Under the provisions of the Coal and Steel Community, a
worker can get his full wages for six months if he is displaced
from his job as a result of the operation of the Common
Market: a pattern for what should be done at national level
to make progress towards economic efficiency acceptable to
the workers. The Investment Bank puts money into the less
developed areas of the Community. A detailed scheme has
been agreed for the introduction of equal pay for women
throughout the Community by 1965. Monnet has shown
what further vistas could be opened up when he advocated
that the resources generated by the Common Market should
finance a huge programme to extend the benefits of higher
education to all Europe's citizens.[1]

The original vision of a union embracing the whole of
Europe was given a great impulse by the British application
to join the Economic Community, followed by those of Den-
mark, Ireland and Norway. As Monnet had predicted, when
they realised that the Community was a fact not a mirage the

[1] Speech by Jean Monnet to the Second European Conference of
Christian Trade Unions, 8-10 May 1962.

British wanted to take part: both for the benefit of the large
single market and in order to share in the political influence
that the Community would develop. The Brussels negotiations
uncovered few problems regarding the entry of Britain itself
into the single market and economic union, apart from the
length of the transitional period for the incorporation of
British agriculture into the Common Market; the problems
almost all concerned the relationship of the enlarged Community with the outside world, which is considered in the next
chapter. The fact that Britain applied to join and that, apart
from these external problems, the Community system raised
few practical impediments must be regarded as further evidence of the Community's success.

More remarkable, though harder to measure, is the political
progress that the Community had made. It has already been
suggested that the dominant political problem of the age is to
create a system within which the nations will live in peace.
The Community had gone very much farther towards solving
this problem for its members than any other international
body or group. In the atmosphere of mutual trust engendered
within the Community framework, it has been difficult to
remember how bitter were the feelings between the French
and the Germans less than twenty years ago. The forces of
extreme nationalism, which naturally thrive on the claustro-
phobic atmosphere of exclusive nation-states, were on the
decline, particularly in Germany. Instead of the sense of
national rivalry and antagonisms, there was a feeling that
peaceful and just solutions would be found for common problems or conflicts of interest; as Monnet has said, the feeling
that such solutions are possible has tended to make them a
fact.

The members had taken important and difficult decisions
in common, particularly in questions of agriculture and the
external tariff. This had given them a belief in their ability to
solve their problems and influence events, in place of the impotence that is too often felt by a nation the size of Britain
in the world today; and this belief was confirmed by the
American decision, made as a response to the new weight of
the Community in world trade, to work for a programme of
tariff cuts on an entirely new scale.

The European Parliament had adopted a draft convention
for strengthening the Community's democratic structure by

means of direct elections to the Parliament and a proposal for creating a Political Community within which, after a transitional period of three years, certain questions of foreign policy would be decided by majority vote. Were it not for de Gaulle's obstruction of all such measures to improve and strengthen the Community, there can be little doubt that the process of building Monnet's Europe would now be continuing. Monnet, in a speech[1] made during the course of the British negotiations, was not being fanciful when he forecast that economic integration would lead to political union in Europe and eventually to Federation.

But de Gaulle is the Head of State in France and, given the weaknesses and incompleteness of the Community that have been described above, he has the power to veto all new initiatives for the building of Monnet's Europe within the framework of the Six. Why he will do so and how his opposition can be overcome or circumvented are considered later. But first it is necessary to examine the posture of Monnet's Europe in the world at large: a posture which de Gaulle opposes even more bitterly than its internal structure.

[1] Speech by Jean Monnet to the Second European Conference of Christian Trade Unions, 8-10 May 1962.

3

MONNET'S REVOLUTION

THERE are now few who contest the benefits that the Community has brought its members in helping to solve their internal problems. De Gaulle, in his doctrinaire hostility to the Community method, is in an almost eccentric minority. But more people, particularly in Britain since the Community's external policies became the crux of the negotiations for British entry, have asked doubtingly whether the Community is good or bad for the world outside.

The question is indeed crucial. If, in this atomic age, the Community were found to be less conducive to world stability and order than its members would be likely to be separately, then it is doubtful whether it could be justified at all, whatever benefits it might bring its members for the time being.

If the Community is largely neutral, neither good nor bad, in its impact on the outside world, then it is greatly to be welcomed for healing Europe's old sores and giving the continent a healthy constitution for the future. Indeed, this laying of the European ghosts that have in this century brought so much trouble to the world could not but be of benefit to everybody, even if Europe were to do no more than avoid stirring up mischief in the world at large.

If on the other hand those people are right who claim, as Monnet himself does, that Community Europe is only the first stage of a process that will spread the Community method across the world, helping to solve problems such as hunger, poverty and the Bomb as it has been helping to solve problems in Europe, then the Community should be a focus for the attention of everybody who is deeply concerned about the condition of the world as a whole.

Community experience: liberal policies; towards a more organised world economy

The Community has shown itself to be liberal, or outward-looking as the jargon has it, in most of the decisions of com-

mercial policy that it has taken. The tariffs on the Rome
Treaty's List G of difficult items were fixed lower than the
average of the four tariffs and much lower than had been
expected. Special provision was made to ease the impact of
moves towards the common outer tariff on countries outside
the Community. The eventual level of the common tariff for
all industrial products was cut by 20 per cent.

The negotiations for British membership raised peculiarly
difficult problems of external policy for a new Community
that had still to make sure of its own cohesion. The British
wanted to ensure that no vital sectors of the Commonwealth's
varied exports to Britain would be substantially damaged
when the common tariff was put round the British market. The Six wanted to avoid any serious weakening in the
structure of common external policies that they were laboriously building up. In these circumstances, and with France,
as the leading member of the Community, nursing a desire to
see the negotiations fail, it is remarkable that fairly satisfactory
solutions had been found for most of the problems of trade
with the less-developed countries of the Commonwealth: full
association offered to the African members; tariff concessions
for the Asians and comprehensive trade agreements to deal
with the problems of their exports to Europe. A formula had
also been found to solve the thorny problem of the agricultural exports of Australia, Canada and New Zealand,
although there would certainly have been considerable difficulties in its application. Thus, except where its farmers were
concerned, in which sector few liberals are available to cast
the first stone, the Community's performance in the British
negotiations had been reasonably helpful and outward-looking.

But just as doctrinaire liberalism and laisser faire are not
enough to deal with Europe's own problems, so more organised solutions are required on the wider scale; and it is here
that the Community has made its most significant mark. The
power of its example and the reflexes of the men who run it
have induced more organised ways of dealing with economic
problems in the world at large.

These innovations have resulted mainly from efforts to meet
problems that inevitably arise when a large Common Market
is established; but if successful they will not only solve those
immediate problems but also permanently improve the conditions under which world trade takes place. Thus the Trade

Expansion Act, passed by the Congress of the United States
as a means to keep trade flowing between America and the
Community while the common tariff was being erected, was
not only unprecedentedly liberal, authorising the President to
negotiate in order to cut tariffs by up to half on all products
and to remove them entirely from those products of which the
Common Market and the United States are the world's dominant suppliers. It has also been shown by the preliminary
negotiations at Geneva that, if de Gaulle does not succeed in
another act of sabotage, tariffs are likely to be cut according
to a general programme akin to the one that was devised for
the cuts within the Community itself, rather than by the piece-
meal method that has made previous GATT negotiations so
complicated and, recently, unrewarding. It has also been indicated that distorting factors other than tariffs will be taken
more into account than in the past : a concession to the Community's principle that the freeing of trade must be accompanied by measures of economic union.

Two of the problems arising out of the British negotiations
brought forth proposals that would have been implemented
had Britain joined and that could have been of general benefit
in dealing with world trade problems in the future. One was
the principle of world commodity agreements. Many United
Nations reports have urged the benefits to be obtained from
such agreements but hitherto they have been applied to only
a few commodities. If the negotiations between Britain and the
Community had succeeded, effective agreements were to have
been applied to many new commodities, thus introducing at
the international level systems of organising commodity markets such as almost all nations already find it necessary to
employ internally in order to safeguard their own farmers.
Such arrangements are urgently needed if developing countries
are not to suffer indefinitely from the prolonged weakness of
commodity markets, which is probably the most potent brake
on their progress.

The British negotiations also threw up the idea of the comprehensive trade agreements that would, after British accession
to the Community, have been negotiated with India, Pakistan,
Ceylon and Malaysia. Pending the conclusion of such agreements, there would have been a guarantee that the level of
these countries' exports to the Community would not fall.
After several years in which the large sums of aid

transferred from the West to the developing countries have been outweighed by the decline of their export earnings, due largely to the above-mentioned weakness of commodity markets, this was a most important innovation; and equally valuable was the reinforcement to the principles of organisation and planning in the field of world trade that the comprehensive trade agreements could have represented.

When the Rome Treaty was negotiated, there was the problem of the trade of the colonies, mostly French territories in Africa, that enjoyed preferential access to the market of one or other of the Six. The French wanted to protect these colonies from damage when the common tariff was erected, just as the British later wished to safeguard the Commonwealth. With the French bargaining position almost impregnable, however, for reasons explained in chapter 2, the French managed to extract from their reluctant partners concessions for these Associated Overseas Countries and Territories (or Associated Overseas States as they are now called, following their independence) that were much greater than were required for the purpose, to the extent of endangering the interests of many other developing countries in Africa, Asia and Latin America which export in competition with the French-speaking countries of Africa. But much of the restrictively preferential character of the system has been removed by cuts in the Community's external tariff on tropical products and the offer of association on the same terms to Commonwealth countries in Africa, made during the British negotiations and still held open. The system that remains, after its amendment in the renewed Convention of Association, contains some features that provide very valuable lessons for the better organisation of the world economy.

Thus tariffs on imports from the associates into the Community are due to be abolished by the same regular and general programme as applies to the internal tariff disarmament. The Six contribute substantial sums to the Development Fund which finances public investments and technical assistance for the associates and is also to support their earnings from commodity exports where these may be damaged by the loss of tariff preference. There is to be a joint parliamentary assembly and a joint council of ministers in which representatives of the associates and the Six will meet on equal terms. All these techniques—regular programmes of tariff reductions by the industrialised countries, regional development funds, support for commodity earnings and institutions in which the advanced and the emergent meet on equal terms—could usefully be more widely applied.

The Latin American Free Trade Area and the Central American Common Market—encouraging steps away from the extreme and autarchic nationalism that has beset the continent in the past—were also set up as a reflection of the EEC.

It is not possible to say how far the methods shown in these various initiatives might anyway have been adopted to solve the problems of world trade and investment, even had the Community never existed. But it seems unlikely that the Americans would have wished to adopt the pattern of general and regular tariff reductions but for the example of the Community, and the influence of Monnet on the American administration's thinking; new commodity agreements have long been in the air but it was Community officials with the British who brought them down to earth; the concept of the comprehensive trade agreement was certainly influenced by the Community methods of thought; the Association of Overseas States was initially all the Community's own work, more recently with the help of the associates; and the Free Trade Area and Common Market in Latin America were directly inspired by the Community pattern. So it seems fair to claim that the Community, by its work and by its example, has helped substantially to introduce valuable new methods into the organisation of the world economy, which might contain the seeds of the fuller application of the Community method later on.

Monnet's revolution: European federation, Atlantic partnership, world order

This is certainly Monnet's view. In his speech to the World Congress of Man-made Fibres, cited earlier, he expressed the belief that the setting aside in Europe of the old attitude of domination in inter-state relations was creating a new mentality and method of action that Europeans would equally apply in their relations with peoples in other continents. After mentioning the Trade Expansion Act, he suggested that common action on a wider than European scale should be undertaken to deal with the problems of monetary stability, world agriculture and aid to underdeveloped areas. Looking further ahead, he envisaged that a united Europe would lead to Atlantic partnership and then to a settlement with Russia : that the consolidation of the West would remove from the Soviet government all hope of ruling by dividing, and thus provide the conditions for a genuine disarmament agreement.

Thus Monnet did not expect that Europe would just add one more great power to the world, but that it would bring its Community method to help solve world problems. "The natural attitude of a European Community based on the exercise by nations of common responsibilities will be to make these nations also aware of their responsibilities, as a Community, to the world. . . . European unity is the most important event in the West since the war, not because it is a new great power, but because the new institutional method it introduces is permanently modifying relations between nations and men. Human nature does not change but when nations and men accept the same rules and the same institutions to make sure that they are applied, their behaviour towards each other changes. This is the process of civilisation itself."[1]

Thus Monnet's Europe is conceived not as an ultimate objective but as the beginning of a process : only a first step, though an essential one. It is essential, for only if there is a thorough-going merger of sovereignty by a balanced and important group of nations is the general process of transcending sovereignty likely to get off the ground. The European Economic Community should lead to a Political Community and eventually a federation, at the same time generating the motive power for creating Atlantic union and eventually world order. The union of Europe, and later of the West, ". . . is not an end in itself. It is the beginning of the road to the more orderly world we must have if we are to escape destruction".[2]

Again, we lack a ready-made word to describe this process, because it is a new one. It is no less than the projection of the pragmatic federalism of Monnet's Europe towards other continents and eventually on to the world plane. After centuries in which nationalism and imperialism have dominated the world, the idea of replacing the absolute power of the nation-state by a system of international democracy on a world-wide

[1] Address by Jean Monnet at the Second World Congress of Man-made Fibres, London, 1 May 1962.
[2] Speech by Jean Monnet at Dartmouth College, USA, 11 June 1961.

scale is so radical as to be revolutionary; and the process is therefore called, in this book, Monnet's revolution.

These are the intentions of Monnet and some of the federalists on the Continent and in Britain. But, it may be asked, are they widely enough supported to have any hope of success?

Although the Europeans represent a wide range of political opinion, there is very strong support among them for the ideas of Atlantic partnership, in the fields of both trade and defence. There can be little doubt that, with governments of the Six that consisted of supporters of the Community idea, such a partnership would readily be evolved.

If the less immediate prospect of a world order based on similar principles is discussed with the average European, he will certainly agree in principle but will probably take the view that this is something with which he can hardly concern himself deeply for the present. As he is already engaged in a gigantic task, which a decade ago most people thought impossible, this is an understandable attitude. Its consequences are that at present, if the average European has his way in the Community, he will act liberally in the world at large and will foster good relations with the United States, but he will not be a conscious agent of Monnet's revolution as a whole. He is, however, instinctively open to Monnet's reasoning and opposed to any narrow chauvinism, and there is therefore a good chance that a Europe run by the Europeans would indeed set in train the process that Monnet describes.

But the governments of the Six are not at present all run by Europeans. France is governed by de Gaulle, who is, for reasons explained in the next chapter, even more hostile to Monnet's revolution than he is to Monnet's Europe. The coming struggle between de Gaulle and the Europeans will probably throw new light on the extent to which the latter will become protagonists of Monnet's revolution. It will certainly be a struggle between those who would make Europe at best a highly beneficent, at worst a neutral, force in world affairs, and a man who would turn the Community into a rogue elephant. This will not happen if the gaullist challenge is properly understood and energetically met, and the next chapter is therefore devoted to its analysis.

4

DE GAULLE'S CHALLENGE

DE GAULLE has shown his distaste for Monnet's Europe from the start. He opposed the creation of the European Coal and Steel Community and his chief lieutenant, Michel Debré was its bitterest critic. De Gaulle was uncompromisingly hostile to the proposal for a European Defence Community and, had it not been for gaullist opposition, the EDC and a European Army would be in existence today. He disliked the Economic Community from the time of its establishment and it now appears that he has tolerated it since his return to power only in order to keep the other members bound to France while he tries to twist it into an old-fashioned alliance under French hegemony.

Since de Gaulle has ruled France, he has constantly blocked new initiatives in the direction of Monnet's Europe. He has continued to emphasise his aversion to the idea of the Communities by repeatedly slighting references to their institutions. He has opposed the Communities' being strengthened by means of a fusion of the three executives and their democratisation by means of direct elections to the European Parliament. He prevented the European University from being established under the aegis of the Community institutions. He had the President of Euratom, M. Hirsch, replaced because Hirsch was following too European a policy. And he has refused to compromise with the other five governments who, with the support of the European Parliament, wanted to found a political union on the Community pattern.

These were Fabian tactics. But de Gaulle has now, by his autocratic use of the veto in the most important issue the Community has yet had to face, openly challenged the principles of Monnet's Europe. He has at the same time, by his exclusion of Britain from the Community and his evident desire to break the growing partnership with America, displayed his hostility to the whole process of Monnet's revolution. This antagonism to Monnet's ideas is no accident;

it is the product of his fundamental instincts and of the political philosophy that stems from them.

De Gaulle against Monnet: autocratic, chauvinist

De Gaulle is an autocrat. His instinct is to dominate those weaker than him; to attack any rivals for power; and, if he cannot dictate his own terms, to refuse to co-operate at all. These traits were shown by his conduct as an ally during the war; by his ruthless ousting of the unfortunate General Giraud from co-leadership in Algeria in 1943; by his abdication from power in 1946 when he disagreed with the political parties about the new constitution; by his contempt for the "classe politique", his destruction of opposition and his exclusively personal conduct of government in the Fifth Republic. They are more amusingly illustrated by two revealing remarks attributed to him: his sardonic "Me voici encore une fois seul", on hearing that Henri Tissot, the comedian, who had won great acclaim in Paris through his parodies of de Gaulle's oratory had now given them up; and his admonition to President Kennedy "Listen only to yourself".

With this impulse to dominate and ingrained contempt for other people, de Gaulle has almost reduced political life in France to the imposition of his own will. Parliament has become a rubber stamp; the courts subject to decisions of the executive; the ministers not really ministers, but rather the heads of departments of the Civil Service. Cabinet meetings apparently consist largely of lectures given by de Gaulle; there is no attempt to form a collective view of important matters. The Prime Minister and Foreign Minister of France were giving assurances that there was no objection to British membership of the Common Market only a few hours before the press conference in which de Gaulle proclaimed his reasons for casting his veto. This was presumably because they did not know of the decision, not because they were telling lies. M. Joxe, one of those closest to de Gaulle, learnt that the Sahara was to be a part of Algeria at one of de Gaulle's press conferences. Joxe was at the time the minister responsible for Algerian affairs. The normal organs of government are treated with contempt; France is ruled instead by personal decision, press conference, television appearance and referendum.

Gaullists claim that the Fifth Republic is fundamentally democratic because it has elections and referenda. Such reasoning is naïve after so many dictators have, in recent times, used elections and referenda as tricks of the trade. Equally essential to democracy are the rule of law, which has been called in question by de Gaulle; the limitation of the executive, which is no longer respected; freedom of the main organs of communication—the French television and radio are instruments of government propaganda; the powers of Parliament, now emasculated; and a whole subsoil and infrastructure of democracy in the activity of local government and of constituency parties and the formation of responsible opinion in all sorts of voluntary groups: in short, all the "intermediaries" between himself and the people that de Gaulle itches to destroy. In undermining all these things, de Gaulle is gravely weakening the democratic political forces in France and increasing the danger that his successors will be an authoritarian regime of the Right or the Communist Party.

It is to be expected that de Gaulle will behave in the Community as autocratically as he does in France, since this behaviour springs from his nature and not from any tactical considerations. "The Gaullist view of the Community's political future is, in fact, the present Fifth Republic writ large—a sobering thought for those who are inclined to view *l'Europe des patries* as a welcome and acceptable philosophy for the future."[1] Experience so far has borne this out.

De Gaulle's contemptuous treatment of his fellow Continentals was shown in the negotiations to form a political union of the Six. Having persuaded Dr. Adenauer in February 1961 to agree to a form of political union to his liking, that is to say without any supranational features, de Gaulle expected the other four members of the Community to accept his text without further discussion—a suggestion that they took very far from kindly. Then after the French negotiators had, through many months of work, made concessions to the point of view of the Five, de Gaulle suddenly withdrew them all and presented the same uncompromising plan as before.

The dictatorial manner in which de Gaulle rejected further negotiations for British membership of the Community needs no emphasis. Professor Hallstein has explained how this action flouted the proper procedures of the Community. "The right

---

[1] Roy Pryce, *The Political Future of the European Community,* Marshbank and the Federal Trust, 1962, p. 55.

of veto is also subject to rules, and it must be used with consideration. It is also necessary to avoid creating the impression that the Community and its aims, the Community institutions and the Community procedure are merely instruments of a country's diplomacy."[1] It is necessary, indeed, not only to avoid creating the impression that this is so, but also to prevent its actually being so. And while de Gaulle rules France, he will try to use the European Community and all other international organisations as instruments of French diplomacy.

Since in the Community de Gaulle is dealing with other states, not as in France with individuals or political parties that are subject to the state power he wields, the means by which he can try to dominate them are more limited. But the weapons of power diplomacy are available: the *diktat*, as in his attempt to foist a gaullist pattern of political union on the Five; the veto; blackmail by threatening the interests of his neighbours, in the case of the Community or other international organisations, by the threat of blocking progress desired by his partners or even of putting the organisation into cold storage or breaking it up; blandishment by means of minor concessions following on a major coup, or of insincere offers such as that of association with the Community for the British, when in fact de Gaulle tried to prevent even a system of regular consultation; the raising of hopes for such things as German reunification; or of fears such as that the Americans will withdraw their protection from Europe.

These Machiavellian techniques have been used by autocrats for centuries. They are the extension to the international plane of the habit of treating other people as tools of power instead of as collaborators. Democratic governments, accustomed to treating people more considerately, have been less inclined to use them, especially in their dealings with each other in the western alliance in recent years. But it is in the European Community that, as Professor Hallstein points out, such methods were being most systematically replaced by better ways of behaviour. A process of international democracy was being evolved which included objective assessment of the general interest, careful discussion of the results, the painstaking composition of wills and, ultimately, the possibility of a decision

[1] Statement by Professor Dr. Walter Hallstein made to the European Parliament on 5 February 1963.

by majority vote. De Gaulle's methods are fundamentally antagonistic to each stage of this process. In the face of what Monnet calls "the process of civilisation itself", they are a return to political barbarism.

If de Gaulle's Caesarism clashes head-on with Monnet's Europe, his other outstanding characteristic does so no less: his chauvinism. Like the bonapartist veteran who gave his name to the word, de Gaulle's mind is filled with "la gloire" to the exclusion of all else. This is the ideological mould for his autocratic instincts: the national power and grandeur of France, incarnated by himself. He sees all nations and political issues through this distorting lens.

This chauvinism pervades his speeches and writings. It is the constant factor in his deeds. It was to be seen during the war in his unceasing quarrels with his allies: in his struggle for territory in Germany, almost as if Britain and America were the enemies of France; in his obsession with the intrigues between himself and the British in the Middle East. He has kept the bulk of French forces out of NATO and undermined the alliance, and virtually withdrawn French support from the United Nations. Now he has flatly rejected collaboration with Britain in economics and with America in defence.

This obsesssion with the power of the French state underlies the theoretical justification for his opposition to the European Communities. ". . . the states . . . are the only entities which have the right to give orders and the power to act. To imagine that something can be built up which can act effectively and be approved by the peoples outside or over and above the states is an illusion."[1] This flatly contradicts, and was intended to contradict, the Community ideal of a union of peoples that breaks down the exclusive authority of the nation-states and creates the beginnings of a common citizenship. It also incidentally belies the recent history of France's largest partners in the Common Market, Germany and Italy; for both these states consist of "something . . . built up . . . over and above" the former small German and Italian states. In calling this an illusion, de Gaulle was showing scant consideration for his closest allies.

During the same press conference, de Gaulle continued: "It is natural that the states of Europe should have at their

[1] Press conference held by General de Gaulle, 5 September 1960.

disposal specialised bodies for the problems they have in common, to prepare and if necessary to follow up their decisions, but these decisions are theirs to take. They can only be theirs, and they can take them only by co-operation."[1] The reader may understandably be confused by this way of putting things. After all, "co-operation" with other members of the Community was not the keynote of de Gaulle's decision to keep Britain out. But de Gaulle's real meaning was that decisions could not be taken without the French government's agreement. The fact that the co-operation of de Gaulle is peculiarly difficult to secure is not relevant to the theory, which is that the power of decision must remain with the national governments. This theory runs directly counter to the Community method whereby common action flows from decisions taken within the Community institutions, in the general interest and where necessary by majority vote.

The fact that de Gaulle's autocratic instincts are clothed in a political theory of nationalism does not make much difference to his own behaviour in the Community. It does, however, increase the danger that this behaviour may become embodied in an authoritarian and nationalist pattern that could outlive him. If de Gaulle was, like many Latin American dictators have been, an opportunist just on his own account, his influence would not survive his political demise. He is, however, an opportunist not for himself but for his conception of France, which naturally can identify much of the French nation with his thinking; and it is possible that his theory of inter-state relations could survive him on the European plane, where the practice of personal autocracy as such would not.

But de Gaulle's chauvinism sets him in conflict most of all with the external posture of Monnet's Europe: with Monnet's revolution and, most violently, with its immediate manifestation of Atlantic partnership.

De Gaulle's evident hostility to America is fed by his envy of American power. His own nature cannot brook a rival in authority; nor is it tolerable to him that France should be weaker than America. Hence his reckless rebuffs to the power on which Europe depends for its defence and his undermining of the economic co-operation on which the prosperity of the West must be based.

Despite the history of Anglo-French rivalry since Joan of

[1] Press conference held by General de Gaulle, 5 September 1960.

Arc and despite the wartime slights that he remembers and the immense debt to Britain that must be even more galling to him, there is no evidence that de Gaulle has any abnormal personal antipathy towards the British. Britain's crime is to be as powerful as France and hence a rival for European leadership—on the gaullist assumption that Community institutions are merely a façade for the domination of Europe by one national power. So Britain has to be weakened by exclusion from Europe in order that France can be on top.

His attitude towards the United Nations is totally destructive and reflects a disdain for the emergent nations that now form its majority. He speaks of the United Nations with withering sarcasm, calling it the "disunited nations" and a "disorganisation", and deploring its "riotous and scandalous" proceedings. He wants it to be reorganised as a concert of great powers in order to exclude the new nations' influence. Like Russia, he has refused not only to pay the French share for the UN operations in the Congo, but also a French contribution to the interest and repayment of the $200 million bond issue that has for the time being saved the United Nations from bankruptcy.

Equally intransigent and dangerous is his policy towards disarmament and test bans. He has been negative on the subject of disarmament and ignores the test ban on the grounds that it would prevent a resurgence of French power. His earlier philosophising about the atomic bombs dropped on Japan might lead one to expect a different policy: "I must say that the revelation of these terrible engines of war moved me right to the bottom of my spirit... but even if I was not surprised I was nonetheless tempted to succumb to despair in seeing the means appear which would perhaps allow men to destroy mankind."[1] But de Gaulle is against a test ban; concern for the future survival of mankind has given place to his consuming ambition to increase the power of France.

It would of course be foolish to claim that all of de Gaulle's policies are bad. But taken as a whole they are intolerable because they are all designed to increase French national power, regardless of any other consequences. This makes some of them dangerous in themselves; and their cumulative effect is to threaten world security and progress towards Monnet's Europe and Monnet's revolution.

[1] General de Gaulle, *Mémoires de Guerre 1944–46*, p. 227, Plon 1959.

Thus de Gaulle has given independence to the French colonies. The reasons for this were explained in his *Mémoires de Guerre:* "in order that the people for whom we are responsible may remain tomorrow with France, it is necessary for us to take the initiative of transforming their condition as subjects into one of autonomy and, into association, those relationships which, at present, are for them only those of dependence".[1] De Gaulle was concerned not with the welfare of the African peoples but with securing allies for France : a perfectly respectable motive in itself, but not one that implies liberal policies towards the emergent nations as a whole. His attitude towards the overwhelming bulk of them that do not speak French is better exemplified by his scorn for the United Nations, mentioned above.

Some left-wing people have believed that de Gaulle is basically progressive, because when he ruled France immediately after the war he introduced many features of a welfare state and nationalised large sectors of the French economy, and because he believes in modern technology. But most dictators, fascist, communist or bonapartist, have used all these techniques. They do so in order to strengthen the state and to unite the nation in its support : to keep up with the international Joneses in terms of prestige and power.

It is not only left-wingers who will applaud a desire to have better relations with Russia. But this drift in de Gaulle's policy assumes a different aspect in the light of the following precept: "Collaborate with the West and the East, where necessary contract alliances with one side or the other" :[2] "where necessary" meaning where this will increase French influence. Thus, whether the political systems of America and Russia are good, bad or indifferent is of no interest to de Gaulle; both are merely factors in the equation by which he hopes to increase French power. Gaullists have claimed that de Gaulle is a good ally because he supported the United States during the Cuban crisis. But the *Mémoires de Guerre* were written after deep reflection at a time of life when basic ideas do not change; and they show that any support for the Western alliance is a temporary expedient, to be abandoned when this seems "necessary" to de Gaulle. Nor would it appear from the tenor of his precept that, if he did change sides, his new friends in the

[1] De Gaulle, *op. cit.,* p. 223.   [2] *Ibid.,* p. 179.

Kremlin could be any more sure of the loyalty of his friend-
ship. Khrushchev's cool reception to gaullist overtures indicates
that they themselves would set little store by it.

De Gaulle is simply not interested in any political ideas
apart from those of the nation-state and of France's precedence among nation-states. Once this is understood, it is easy to
explain his lack of moral commitment in the East-West conflict; his simultaneous spurning of Britain and wooing of
Franco; his abhorrence of any thought of controlling the
power of nation-states within a system of international democracy. His opposition to Monnet's Europe and Monnet's
revolution is complete and unalterable, based on a fundamental conflict of political philosophies: autocracy against
democracy; chauvinism against liberalism; power against welfare; man as the servant of leviathan instead of political institutions in the service of man.

De Gaulle's Europe: confusion or confidence trick

De Gaulle is opposed to Monnet's ideas. But he is not in
politics just to spite Monnet. He has a positive programme to
assert the position of France in the world, the broad lines of
which can now be deduced with what is probably fair
accuracy.

The first phase in this programme is the creation of a
French hegemony on the continent of Europe. De Gaulle
realises that French power alone is too slender a basis for a
leading role in the world. His first need therefore is to gather
around him other nations that are weak enough to be dominated by France yet together strong enough to stand on equal
terms with Russia and America. "Form a group, from the
political, economic and strategic points of view, of the states
that border the Rhine, the Alps and the Pyrenees."[1] The
European Community, shorn of any supranational powers,
seemed tailor-made to the purpose, and Germany, with its
industrial strength and diplomatic weakness, the necessary
centre-piece.

The pattern of this policy is uninhibitedly described in a
document whose text was published in the Belgian press[2] and
was stated to be that of a memorandum sent on 29 August
1960 by M. Peyrefitte, the chief gaullist expert on European

[1] De Gaulle, *op. cit.*, p. 179.
[2] *La Dernière Heure*, 9 February 1962.

affairs, to M. Debré. The document has been repudiated by
the French authorities but it seems to describe accurately
enough the essence of gaullist policy. One of the "imperative
conditions" of French policy in Europe would be "not to give
the impression that France wishes to exclude Britain, but
nevertheless to adopt the method used by the British after the
war, of dominating the Continental powers through inter-
governmental organisations". The possession of a nuclear
deterrent by France, the only member of the European Community with these weapons, would ensure continued French
predominance among the Six. The insistent gaullist demand
for a European Political Union based on the unanimity principle and with the veto provision is consistent with the document. Nor is it belied by the recent French offer to put the
French deterrent, such as it is, at the service of such a union.
For is it to be supposed that, in a union based on unanimity,
de Gaulle would allow five foreign vetoes on the French
deterrent's use? Or would five foreign fingers each be allowed
to press the button independently? Either of these ideas is out
of the question; it is only possible to believe that de Gaulle will
continue to control the button himself.

Since the Five refused to agree to such a union, de Gaulle
made use of Dr. Adenauer's single-minded devotion to the
cause of Franco-German reconciliation to secure, as a substitute, the Franco-German Treaty. In ratifying it the Germans
have made clear, in a preamble, that this Treaty does not detract in any way from their loyalty to the European Community and to NATO; but the provision for France and Germany to consult and, where possible, to agree on all aspects of
foreign policy was undoubtedly an attempt by de Gaulle to
substitute an inter-governmental system under his domination
for the existing methods of collaboration among the Six and
in the Atlantic alliance.

If in this way he secured a hegemony on the Continent, de
Gaulle could eject American influence and, relying on fear of
China to drive the Russians into his arms, create his concert
of European powers from the Atlantic to the Urals. France
would be the fulcrum for Western Europe; Western Europe
the fulcrum for all of the advanced industrial nations; and de
Gaulle, or his successor, as ruler of France, would have his
hand on a lever of power that would control the world. "Make
of this organisation [the above-mentioned group of Contin-

ental states] one of the three world powers and, if it is necessary one day, the arbiter between the Soviet and Anglo-Saxon
camps."[1]

Because the formation of a European group is the first stage
of de Gaulle's plans, just as it is of Monnet's, some people
have been led to believe that the two men are basically after
the same thing. In fact, they have nothing more in common
than lions and Christians : they share the same arena for the
time being. The difference between their political concepts has
already been analysed in this chapter. Their policies are
equally antithetical. De Gaulle wants an old-style coalition in
Europe led by France, Monnet a democratic Community in
which no one people would predominate. De Gaulle consequently wants Britain out of Europe; Monnet wants Britain in.
De Gaulle wants to sever the links with America; Monnet to
build them into a stronger partnership. De Gaulle hopes to
bargain with Russia independently of America; Monnet on
the basis of the Atlantic partnership. De Gaulle aims ultimately at a world balance of power in which Europe, and
hence France, would come out on top; Monnet at a system of
world order based on the Community method.

De Gaulle's aims are objectionable not only because they
are based on power and domination instead of on order and
democracy, but also because they are too far divorced from
practical possibilities. It seems likely, in view of de Gaulle's
character and the evolution of gaullist policy, that the *Europe
des patries* is intended to be dominated by France. In this case
the talk of a "European Europe" and of an independent deterrent for "Europe" is a confidence trick. But if his intention
were to be realised, it would at least be an alliance of a type
as workable as the present Western alliance : operating after
a fashion because of the clear leadership of one member :
France playing the part that de Gaulle so resents America's
playing now. The chances of the Germans and other Continentals agreeing to an alliance on gaullist lines are considered
in the next chapter and concluded to be slim. But if they did
agree, the alliance would not be dominated by France for
long. Germany and perhaps Italy would become too powerful
for that. Thus there would be two or three nations on an
equal footing. Would they consistently arrive unanimously at
clear and practical decisions? In view of the record of such

[1] De Gaulle, *op. cit.*, p. 179

coalitions, this is not to be believed. What is to stop the group from falling apart? Would Germany smoothly take over the leadership from France? There is no indication whether de Gaulle himself has any clear idea of how his *Europe des patries* could be made to work; one can only suppose that, if it is not intended as a confidence trickster's euphemism for a French hegemony, it is no more than a confusion behind bold phrases. Or would the group evolve into the only other cohesive form : a Political Community based on the majority vote?

This is the hope that has led some Europeans to be covert supporters of de Gaulle : the hope that, although de Gaulle's ways may be rather rough and some of his ideas have an antique air, his powerful will can weld together a European group that will eventually turn into a European Community.

In politics, however, the ends do not justify the means; the means fashion the ends. A group organised by autocratic methods with chauvinistic policies would probably degenerate into a group of squabbling nations that would soon fall apart. The Community has not got so far as this, but there are signs that it could happen if there was another performance such as the veto on Britain. The chauvinism of one member tends to breed nationalist reactions in the others, rather than a general European chauvinism. Indeed, de Gaulle seems to have tried deliberately to stir up a new German nationalism. Peyrefitte's reputed memorandum had reasoned that : "Germany which still keeps its hero cult is ready to show its enthusiasm for a soldier who refuses to accept the decline of the West." A visit to Germany by General de Gaulle and a direct appeal to the German people were therefore recommended. "Such a visit would result in a triumph." This line of thinking explains de Gaulle's tour of Germany in which he made an open appeal to German nationalism, summed up in the phrase "du grosses deutsches Volk". Leading German policians themselves since the war have scrupulously avoided any such incitement of their people.

The consequences of de Gaulle: Western stagnation, American hegemony, Russian hegemony; or back to Monnet's Europe

Suppose, however, that it was possible to incite a European nationalism on chauvinistic lines. De Gaulle could then achieve

his second objective of ousting American influence from
Europe. But the third objective of a coalition of European
powers including Russia, this ramshackle combination of the
Holy Alliance and the Yellow Peril: could that be made to
work? To believe it leaves out of account the dictates of communist ideology. Since the war, the Western alliance has con-
founded Marxist predictions of conflict between the "imperialists"; Marxist dogma has been adapted and a softer line has
resulted in Russia's relations with the West. A deep cleavage
within the capitalist camp would revive the old doctrines and
a hard line would almost inevitably follow. But the facts of
power are still more inimical to the idea of a separate gaullist
deal with Russia. Unless Europe were organised as a central-
ised dictatorship on fascist lines, it would not have the resources to stand on its own against Russia for some decades
to come. Any gap between the departure of America and the
achievement by Europe of such power could be used by Russia
to secure for itself a European hegemony. De Gaulle's vision
of a Europe from the Atlantic to the Urals would then have
come true: but centred on Moscow not on Paris.

But, as is argued in the next chapter, de Gaulle's "success"
in securing the command of Europe, pushing out the Americans, and thus bequeathing to his successors either a powerful,
chauvinistic European nation or, more plausibly, a Europe
dominated by Russia is not a likely prospect. More probable is
either a fairly quick return to the construction of Monnet's
Europe or a longer period in which, without achieving any of
his objectives, de Gaulle yet manages to stymie any real progress in the West. In the latter case, with the Five poised
uneasily between their loyalty to the idea of the European
Community of the Six and legally bound by it to France on
the one hand, and their desire not to cut adrift from the
Western alliance on the other, the West would be stagnant,
failing to organise itself to cope with the great problems that
confront it in defence and even more in economics; the Soviet
bloc would be making the running in the peaceful competition
with the West. After some years of this, the demise of de
Gaulle would probably be followed by an American hegemony over Europe which might or might not stop the rot; in
such circumstances the European nations, discontented because of their lack of real influence, would be reluctant col-

laborators, grudgingly providing less than they should to the combined efforts of the West. The great hope must remain, therefore, that the European nations will return before long to the construction of Monnet's Europe and of Atlantic partnership, to be followed by the further stages of Monnet's revolution. The rest of this book examines how this can be brought about.

There is, then, a fair prospect that de Gaulle will fail within the next few years and that the progress of Monnet's revolution will be resumed. If it is not, the most likely consequence will be a period of stagnation for the West, with a correspondingly greater chance that the communists will eventually win over the world and with the virtual certainty, meanwhile, of that American hegemony over Europe which it is de Gaulle's over-riding ambition to avoid. Alternatively, de Gaulle succeeds in winning Europe and driving out America, with the possible result of a chauvinistic Europe able to play power politics against all comers, but the strong probability of a Russian hegemony in Europe, again leading towards Soviet domination of the world.

Thus the results of de Gaulle's political adventures will be either a most perilous success or ignominious failure: the penalty for trying to be Napoleon in Hitler's century. For the European nations are now too weak for a Napoleon; de Gaulle is playing power politics without power. If he did drive Europe into manufacturing, in time, weapons of mass destruction and means of delivery as powerful as those of Russia and America, then he would be playing a game in which the forfeit is not Waterloo but Armageddon.

The Times has suggested that de Gaulle is a political seer, comparing him with Charles Ellis who invented the game of rugby by picking up the football and running with it. When de Gaulle's conception of French policy has been right, as in 1940 and in the last stages of the Algerian crisis, his inflexible courage has indeed been a great boon. But his flouting of the rules is no longer done in a good cause; it is not inventive, it is atavistic. To resurrect the demon of national power in place of the new principle of international democracy is not like inventing rugby; it is like abandoning the Queensberry rules, throwing away one's boxing gloves and putting on knuckle dusters instead. It is reckless stupidity.

During the Algerian putsch on which de Gaulle rode back to power, students marched through Paris chanting "Soustelle au poteau" and demanding similar treatment for other Algerian leaders. For de Gaulle they had an interesting variation : "de Gaulle au musée". Yes, a museum is the right place for a dinosaur; such a creature would be very dangerous at large in the modern world.

PART II

THE WEST'S RESPONSE

5

EUROPE'S RESPONSE

PART I has depicted the conflict in Europe between two opposite principles, personified by Jean Monnet and General de Gaulle: Monnet's Europe which is liberal, democratic, humane, its first embodiment the three European Communities, its future prospects a European federation, an Atlantic partnership and, it may reasonably be hoped, a developing world order based on Community principles; de Gaulle's which is authoritarian and chauvinist, based on the pursuit of power for the French state, hostile to America, contemptuous of international organisations whether the European Communities or the United Nations, and likely, as long as it obstructs the progress of Monnet's Europe, to undermine the West's ability to help solve the vast and terrible problems that confront the world.

Neither of these principles can progress without the support of the heart of Europe. Monnet's Europe, in order to ensure its democratic balance, requires as a minimum the Five with France or Britain as Germany's counterweight. De Gaulle needs Germany at least, if he is to play power politics with Russia and America; and if he had Germany in tow, Italy and Benelux would find it hard to stand aside.

Whichever principle the Continent espouses will have great power for good or evil in the world. Western Europe is, with America and Russia, one of the world's three great industrial complexes, and it will be decades before another such can grow elsewhere. Nowadays military power and the ability to contribute to the world's economic welfare both depend on industrial strength. The principles for which this strength is used are therefore a factor that will do much to decide the future of the world. This is the background against which Europe's response to the challenge of de Gaulle must be seen.

47

Confusion after the veto: the veto legal, Britain weak, the Five unready

When de Gaulle cast his veto on Britain there was furore among the Europeans. They bitterly resented his autocratic methods; they were deeply suspicious of the anti-American drift of his policies. The storm of fury passed, however, leaving de Gaulle riding smugly high and Britain still outside. Why?

In the first place, the veto was legally de Gaulle's to cast. The Rome Treaty, as one of the concessions to the national sovereignty of its existing members, provides that they must unanimously agree to the accession of new ones. As Professor Hallstein said, de Gaulle ignored the proper Community procedures for reconciling divergent points of view, but had the negotiations continued he would legally have been entitled to employ his veto in the end.

In these circumstances, the only way in which the Five could try to get the decision reversed was by political pressure: by witholding from de Gaulle, or threatening to withold, things that he wanted for France. Thus there was talk of one or other of the Five blocking measures proposed in the Community that were of interest to France: progress in agricultural policy; a decision on the "financial contribution" whereby food importers, *i.e.* mainly Germany, would pay for the support of Community farmers, many of them in France; the new arrangements for the Association of Overseas States; a special status for Algeria. But it is very doubtful whether economic sanctions would have had any effect on de Gaulle except, perhaps, to encourage him to disrupt or leave the Community. He is not interested in *l'intendance*, as he slightingly refers to economic questions; economics are, he implies, the quarter-master's branch for the statesman who is concerned with frontiers, political treaties, the power of the state and its rank in world affairs.

The only reprisal which might, therefore, have caused him to withdraw his veto would have been a German refusal to ratify the Franco-German Treaty. Dr. Adenauer as Chancellor, however, was almost as suspicious of British entry into the Community as de Gaulle; and the German parties were not willing to endanger what they saw as the crowning of the patient years of Franco-German reconciliation and to risk a trial of strength with de Gaulle that might destroy the European Community, in what might well be a fruitless attempt to get the veto withdrawn.

The reluctance of the Five to face a showdown was much influenced by the long hesitations and final doubts of the British about membership of the Community. Through the 'fifties Britain had stood coldly aside from its construction and British policies were not, to say the least, contrived to help the work. When Britain finally did apply to join, her government equivocated about the political implications; the Labour Party developed a strongly negative attitude; the Gallup polls eventually showed a third of the country for entry, a third undecided and a third against; and the British negotiators marked time for three crucial months before the veto, during which the government took a sudden step away from Europe at Nassau. Many of the Europeans found it hard to believe that Britain would be a good member of the Community and some thought that she would be a disruptive force.

These suspicions, if understandable, were almost certainly unjust. Monnet, in a newspaper interview after the rupture of the negotiations, dealt with the question of British "ripeness for the Community" as follows: "When European integration began in 1950 the Six were far from desiring or agreeing to all that has been done since. I have no doubt that if Britain had come into the Community on the same terms as the other member-countries, subject to the same rules, participating in the same institutions and sharing the same common interests, she would have consolidated her own European evolution and reinforced ours."[1] The British as a whole, including the Labour Party, had made up their minds that, if they entered the Community, they would help to make it work. As Monnet suggests they would also probably have come to accept the idea of a Political Community; nor is it likely that they would have impeded progress more than gaullist France. If, however, the French had returned to federalist ways before the British developed so far, the Six might well have proceeded with a Political Community on their own, leaving the British to catch that bus too at a later stop.

But it is one thing to be a good member in a going concern; it is another to share in constructing a Community from the

[1] Interview with Jean Monnet, published in the *Corriere della Sera*, 7 April 1963.

ground upwards, especially if this is the reconstruction of a shattered Community whose members have therefore lost much of their confidence. It would be hard to claim that, in early 1963, the British as a whole gave grounds for faith in their will to do this or in the requisite understanding of the federalist nature of the Community process which would enable them to do it. Thus the Europeans were justifiably doubtful whether, if France left the Community, Britain could step in and help to reconstruct the Community's rules and institutions, with their essentially federal nature.

De Gaulle, for his part, made full use of these weaknesses in the British position, of the doubts that they engendered in the Europeans' minds and of the indispensability thus accorded to France. Using, as one trained in military methods, the weapon of surprise, he forced the issue before the Five and the Europeans expected it. They had no previous experience of an all-out attack on the Community's collective methods. They were unprepared and for some months they drifted without a coherent policy to combat and repulse militant gaullism. It would be quite wrong, however, to jump to the conclusion that Monnet's Europe is checkmated by de Gaulle, or for the excluded British to change their euphoric post-veto soubriquet of the "friendly Five" into a disillusioned and sarcastic "feeble Five". Monnet's Europe has been checked; but the policies for its defence and its resurgence are beginning to emerge.

Defending, then relaunching Monnet's Europe: apply the Treaties; Community initiatives; no union on gaullist lines

It has been explained why a policy of blocking all measures of interest to France was rejected by the Europeans as a means of retaliation against the veto. All that came of this idea was a delay in signing the renewed provisions for the Association of Overseas States with the Community and a hardening of the German attitude on agriculture. At present the Five seem no more willing to indulge in the opposite pole of policy: virtual submission to all of de Gaulle's demands. Only time, however, and the behaviour of all concerned, particularly the Europeans, the Americans and the British, can tell whether this resolution will be maintained. Meanwhile policy at governmental level is taking the shape

of the package deal and, among the Europeans, of defending
then relaunching Monnet's Europe.

The doctrine of the package deal was outlined by Dr.
Schroeder in a keynote speech to the Community's Council of
Ministers. The other members were tired of making down
payments in the form of concessions to de Gaulle against
French IOUs in the form of understandings that future concessions, such as in the entry of Britain into the Community,
would be made by France. Since these IOUs had not been
honoured, the only valid policy for the future would be to
insist on package deals in which the concessions would be
made simultaneously.

The package that the Six are at present trying laboriously
to wrap up is agreement on agricultural policy and on a
liberal policy in the GATT negotiations, arising out of the
American Trade Expansion Act, to cut tariffs by up to half.
The agricultural policy would be good for the French farmer
and bad for the German one; the tariff cuts in co-operation
with America are much desired by the Five and distasteful to
France. Liberal tariff cuts would be a really valuable concession because they would do much to counter the danger that
de Gaulle will open a rift between Europe and America.
There is not at present any other readily discernible French
concession of similar value that would stand a chance of
being accepted by de Gaulle.

Some Europeans criticise the doctrine of the package on
the grounds that it abandons the concept of the general interest which is at the heart of the European Community.
There is some truth in this. But when one member uses the
"national" aspects of the Community, such as the veto, to
pursue its own ends without regard for the interest of the
others, they cannot refrain from defending themselves. How
much progress is retarded by package deals that balance the
accounts at every stage depends on how exactly they are
balanced. There has been a strong element of the package
deal in certain phases of the Communities' progress in the
past. It is to be feared that Gaullist rigidity will make such
deals harder to transact in the future. But the Five cannot be
blamed for this if the only alternative policy is one of submission, which is unacceptable.

At the same time as the governments have been thinking in
terms of bargaining in packages, the Europeans have been

evolving a strategy for defending and, when possible, re-launching Monnet's Europe. A part of this was explained by Monnet in his interview with the *Corriere della Sera*, referred to on page 49; other aspects emerge from policy documents of the European Movement and the federalist groups in various European countries.

The first principle is to insist that the existing Treaties are applied. De Gaulle is reluctant to break a Treaty but he would be delighted to be able to evade the supranational aspects of the Communities, which are the very heart of them, on the grounds that the Treaties had already been broken by somebody else. The Europeans are therefore in a strong position if the Five adhere punctiliously to the Treaties and de Gaulle is therefore forced to comply too, or openly to renege on France's obligations.

Of course this does not mean that the Five should be black-mailed into policies they think wrong by the fear that, unless they obey, de Gaulle will not apply the Treaties. Nor should they be deterred from using their powers under the Treaty to secure French compliance with policies that they deeply believe to be right. The shock of the veto has misled some people to look on the Communities as a trap within which the other members are prisoners of gaullist policy. But the veto is in fact an exceptional provision. It applies to the admission of new members; and it applies to certain matters until the completion of the second stage of the transitional period, which is due at the end of 1965. At that time the qualified majority begins to apply to many of them, including the key sectors of policy, agriculture and the external tariff, so that the Treaty provides for de Gaulle to be a prisoner of Community policies, not vice versa. Most of the other main aspects of economic, financial, monetary, fiscal and social policy, and also the harmonisation of laws, are matters for unanimity, but not the veto-ridden brand of unanimity where nothing can be done if one member disagrees. If, in any of these sectors, the other Five differ from de Gaulle, there is nothing in the Treaty to prevent them from agreeing separately among themselves if necessary or with outside countries such as the United States or Britain.

De Gaulle has repeatedly said that the Community institutions cannot decide matters of policy, which must be reserved to the national governments. "Any system consisting in the

transfer of our sovereignty to international bodies would be
incompatible with the rights and the duties of the French
Republic.... This renunciation by the European states and in
particular by France would inevitably result in subordination
to foreign interests."[1] This is certainly a threat to disregard
decisions taken against him by majority vote in matters
he thinks important. Whether he would in fact disregard
them or even leave the Community remains to be seen, provided that his threats do not frighten the others into for-
going the weapon of the majority. If they are so frightened,
then it will become true that the Community is a trap for the
Five, but it will be a trap which they themselves have sprung.

It would likewise require some determination on the part of
other members to collaborate with, say, America in monetary
policy in the face of French opposition, for the Treaty enjoins
the Six to try to co-operate among themselves and they would
therefore be obliged to have some unpleasant meetings with
the French representative in order to establish whether there
was a basis for co-operation, before going ahead with any
schemes on a wider scale. But it would be futile to make policies on the assumption that the Five will be too weak to act if
necessary without France in such questions; or that they will
lack the resolution to use their majority vote after the end of
1965 to cut the external tariff, if to do so involved an important issue of principle and all attempts to reach agreement
with France had failed. For to assume this would be to con-
cede defeat before the struggle had begun.

So long as the Five have this much resolution, the Communities, with their provision for majority vote in certain
essential matters and the very restricted powers of veto, are
towers of strength in the building of Monnet's Europe. Their
destruction by any hand but de Gaulle's would be a disaster,
because it would enable him to eliminate all traces of Monnet's Europe, without incurring the odium of doing so and
hence without hardening resistance against him into a determination to rebuild the Communities as soon as possible.

The next principle of European policies is to take new initiatives in the direction of Monnet's Europe. Many of these
would undoubtedly be vetoed by de Gaulle : all those implying an extension of the Community principle of majority
voting, for example, whether in the creation of a European

[1] Television broadcast by General de Gaulle, 19 April 1963.

Political Community or a Defence Community, or in bringing
monetary and economic policies within the majority voting
sector of the Economic Community; and those providing for
more democratic control over the Communities, for example
by giving the European Parliament powers of legislation,
budgetary control and executive appointments. But it is a
good thing to court de Gaulle's vetoes. Too often in the past
he has been able to accuse his opponents of negativism because, in order not to exacerbate relations, they have refrained
from proposing what they thought would be unacceptable to
him, while he has taken a delight in proposing what he knew
was anathema to them, in order to make them either negative
or humiliated, or both. From now on the Europeans should
take the initiative and compel de Gaulle either to accept their
policies or to be clearly seen as the obstruction and thus to
tarnish the image of the great European "Sauveur" that he
seems to have impressed upon the mind of the less sophisticated French voter. Tactics such as these had happily been
forgotten in the atmosphere of goodwill in which the Communities worked; but they are necessary if the gaullist threat
is to be effectively countered.

Other initiatives that the Europeans can take concern the
outward-looking aspects of Monnet's Europe. The Five have
already done this in securing, despite de Gaulle's objections,
regular consultations between Ministers of Britain and the Six.
The tariff negotiations in GATT are another case, but
by the time they are finished, 1966 will be near and the veto
on the Community's tariff decisions will be a swiftly wasting
asset. Collaboration with the United States in defence is not,
of course, subject to any gaullist veto, and the concept of a
multilateral force represents a step towards a European Defence Community in partnership with America; preliminary
moves towards partnership could likewise be made in the
monetary field. In respect to the Community's relations with
the developing countries, some Europeans have suggested that
those concessions agreed for such countries during the British
negotiations should anyway be put into effect, and this has
been done in the offer of association to Commonwealth
countries in Africa and the suspension of the tariffs on tea and
tropical hardwoods in particular.

The third principle of European policy is "no political or
defence union on gaullist lines" or, more crudely, "no new

vetoes". De Gaulle will undoubtedly try to secure agreement
on such a union without majority votes and with the power
of veto, at least on the entry of new members. A union along
these lines has been resisted by the Five during the past two
years, and it would be a triumph for de Gaulle if they were to
weaken now. How much of a triumph depends on the union's
exact form. Periodical discussions between Heads of State or
Ministers might not in themselves do much harm; the
damage is in proportion to de Gaulle's ability to hamstring
co-operation with America or Britain, and this in turn depends
partly on the extent of the veto power. Similar reasoning
applies to the proposals for a monetary union of the Six. The
right principle is to reject all proposals for union without provision for majority votes; and it would be a grave error if the
Five agreed to set up a union and conceded the power of veto
on any important matter.

The whole purpose of this programme of applying the
existing Treaties, taking initiatives towards Monnet's Europe
and refusing to agree to any gaullist union of states is, of
course, to keep intact the foundation for the relaunching of
Monnet's Europe and to bring forward the day when that
will be possible. But meanwhile the Europeans must resign
themselves to a succession of vetoes from de Gaulle. Is there
any quick way by which these vetoes can be by-passed? If
they are not, will the Five have the will and the nerves to
stand firm and resist gaullism for a long period? And if so,
how will the veto eventually be beaten and the progress of
Monnet's revolution resumed?

De Gaulle versus the Europeans: the Five will resist for a time

In trying to overcome resistance among the Five, de Gaulle
will continue to use the weapons of power diplomacy. He will
endeavour to have the advantage of surprise, although this
will not be so easy a second time. He will aim to keep the
Europeans uncertain and divided by riding as far as possible
the European as well as the nationalist horse, and thus weaken
their opposition. He will offer concessions to the Europeans
that may delight some of the more gullible but will not change
the position in any fundamental way; for example: direct
elections to a powerless parliamentary assembly; a merger of
the executives of the three Communities, long wanted by the
Europeans and a useful measure in itself, but nothing to

justify substantial counter-concessions to the gaullist view; and a European defence union in which the other members are offered a guarantee of the protection of the French bomb, such as it is, and the opportunity to express to de Gaulle their views about the circumstances in which he should press the button, but in which there is no provision for a Community system of government.

He will continue to play on the hopes of German reunification and the passions of German nationalism and on the fears of those who want to avoid the break-up of the Communities. He will do his utmost to keep Britain out of Europe and to loosen the ties with America, in order that the Continentals will be more dependent on him and will, like the French, resign themselves to his rule because there is "pas d'alternative".

The Five have a number of weaknesses in the face of this skilful and determined attack. On the Right, among the class of people who formerly supported fascism, there is strong support for his atavistic style of nationalism and hostility to America. A softness towards his policies spreads fairly far towards the centre in some of the countries. Those democratic forces that want to resist him tend to lack coherence and initiative, especially since the French "classe politique", from which so many of the Europeans' leading figures have been drawn, is in eclipse.

On the other hand, there has been a stiffening of the attitude in Germany, which is the key to de Gaulle's plans, with Schroeder's doctrine of the package deal, the addition to the Franco-German Treaty of the preamble stressing the supremacy of the European Community and North Atlantic Treaties, agreement in principle to join with America in a multilateral force, and the decision that Dr. Erhard will succeed Adenauer as Chancellor in 1963. Although the centre-left forces in Italy have been weakened in the recent elections, they still represent a substantial factor of resistance to gaullism. So does a large part of opinion in the Low Countries. And Monnet is still indefatigable. Thus the Five will hold out against gaullism at least for a time; and even if, after a year or two, they were to agree, in default of any alternative initiative, to regular political consultations with de Gaulle, there would certainly be a further period in which those consultations would not greatly reduce their commitment to the European Communities and the Atlantic alliance.

**Beating the veto: try to influence the French; collaborate with
America; Britain should be available**

As we have seen, in order to prevent domination of the
Community by one country and hence a denial of its democratic principles, either France or Britain was necessary as a
counterweight to Germany. Britain was not available so
France was essential, and the economic Communities of the
Continental Six were established. It is natural to expect that
the extension of the Community method to apply to new
fields such as foreign policy and defence, as well as its more
complete and democratic application in the Economic Community, should take place in the same group. The first place
in which to look for progress is therefore France : in a change
in the French policy of vetoing new steps towards Monnet's
Europe.

Is there any chance that de Gaulle will alter his policies
towards Monnet's Europe so far as to accept major reforms
of the Economic Community in a federal direction, or the
establishment of a Political Community or a Defence Community along similar lines? It seems most unlikely, since his
opposition is, as explained in chapter 4, of a fundamental
nature. If it happens, it will be only because he sees that
France will clearly lose all influence in Europe unless he
complies; and this would occur, it is argued below, only if
there was a serious prospect that Britain would establish a
Defence Community of federal character with the Five.

If de Gaulle does not change, how long will he be President of France and what will be the policies of France 'après
de Gaulle'?

Presidential elections are due in 1965, although they could
be brought forward if the Parliament agreed. It is not known
whether de Gaulle will stand again but not at all impossible.
Much could depend on how sure he feels of winning at that
time.

At present the bulk of the electorate is for de Gaulle. He
was the only one who could overcome the Algerian crisis; he
did, for a time at least, mesmerise the Germans; he has got
the better of various foreigners, including the British, after a
succession of national defeats and disasters spread over a
period of forty years; he has defied the Americans and got
away with it; he has restored some order to economic life and

the public believes that its prosperity, much of which is the
fruit of progress in the Fourth Republic, is due to de Gaulle.
He has for the time being destroyed all effective opposition
save the communists (who in fact refrain from real opposition because de Gaulle is doing the work of Moscow in the
Western alliance). Thus he is supported for reasons of national
pride, of his reputation as the *Sauveur*, because there is *pas
d'alternative*, and above all because he has given France a
stability that it has not known for a generation.

There are various sectors of the French people who oppose
him : the workers when they feel their economic interests to
be threatened; a large section of the French establishment
which resents his autocratic use of power; the bulk of the
Army, where hatred of him has always been widespread and
particularly so since the Algerian settlement; and many of the
intellectuals, who oppose him on grounds of democratic principle, and whose views usually in the long run permeate
French society, with its deep respect for learning and culture.

There is also a number of factors that work against him. He
is now seventy-two. There will eventually be a reaction
against personal rule and the destruction of political life in
France. It is not easy for one man to rule a modern state,
especially when he understands little of economics. His
politique de grandeur will be a continuing and excessive
burden on the French economy. The French people have an
exceptionally critical nature and it is hard for a man to keep
their allegiance for long. But none of these things seems
likely to come to a head for several years. The factor that
might perhaps cause public esteem to sink fast would be
the obvious collapse of his external policies : disappointment
at a failure of French influence on the Continent; just possibly, though for any electorate this is a hard thing to understand, aided by a realisation that the undermining of the
political, economic and defence arrangements of the free
world will in the long run be as bad for the French as for
anybody.

All these things will probably be too slow in working themselves out to prevent de Gaulle from being re-elected in 1965
if he wants. In the past, it has been true to say that if he felt
the French people in general to be against him, de Gaulle
would relinquish power. By now, however, he may have
developed "listening only to himself" to the point where he

would ignore the state of mind of the public, just as he has avoided making speeches in big cities since he was barracked on one of his earlier tours. So de Gaulle may be there until the end of a second term as President in 1972.

Could gaullism outlast de Gaulle? De Gaulle's regime is encouraging an authoritarian outlook to grow in a certain type of technocrat, and this could be the basis of a machine that would endure. After all, the French Communist Party has maintained its monolithic strength for quite a long time. Such an outcome does, however, seem unlikely against the fissiparous tendencies of French political life, and it may reasonably be hoped, though it is by no means certain, that authoritarians of Right or Left will be rejected and that democratic forces will rise again.

Thus de Gaulle may be there for two years or for nine, and gaullist policies in Europe might outlast him for a number of years but are not likely to. Whether he changes his policies, and when the French people change him, depend to a substantial degree on the behaviour of the Five and especially the Germans; and this in turn depends significantly upon what the Americans and the British do.

The role of America is considered in chapter 6. The Americans can do much by holding open the offer of partnership. While the full concept of partnership is not realisable without a strong European pillar resolved to collaborate with America, measures such as a multilateral force and the patient pursuit of tariff negotiations with the Six can do much to keep the Five, and especially the Germans, attached to the Atlantic alliance and hence detached from the ambitions of de Gaulle.

The contention of this book is, however, that it is Britain that has the power to turn the tables on de Gaulle, if she has the will. If Britain is available for the Economic Community, in the sense of being held by the Europeans to be a sound enough member to step in and enable the Communities to work if France should one day walk out, then the Five can afford to be stronger in resisting gaullist blackmail than they could if there was no alternative to France, and braver in applying their right of majority vote if necessary. But in order to fill this role of "credibly available alternative" the British will have to develop much farther in their support of the whole concept of Monnet's Europe, that is to say in a federalist sense, than they have done so far despite the great movement of British opinion in favour of the Community idea in the last three years.

Much more dramatically and more swiftly, the British could transform the situation in Europe by offering to put the whole of their defence effort, with those of the Continentals who agreed to do so, into a European Defence Community, broadly on the pattern of the existing European Communities. All of the Six except France did agree, ten years ago, to establish a European Defence Community. The Italians and Benelux countries would almost certainly agree to this now and the Germans might well do so. In these circumstances de Gaulle would have either to bring France in as well or to see his influence on the Continent melting rapidly away. With France in or France out, a great step forward would have been taken in the direction of Monnet's Europe: a European Defence Community and, necessarily, a European Political Community to control the defence effort.

But this depends, even more than "availability" for the Economic Community, on the British deciding that the Community method is sound for defence as it is for economics. In short, it depends on a thorough-going conversion of the British people to the ideas of Monnet. If this happens, it will change the whole structure of European politics to the extent that de Gaulle would be seen almost as a comic anachronism rather than a monstrous incubus on the back of the Western world. The Europeans in France and in the Five would have new heart in them; resistance to gaullist initiatives would come easily; and a quick way would be opened up to the resumption of progress towards Monnet's Europe and Monnet's revolution.

6

AMERICAN SUPPORT

America for Monnet's Europe: constant support; common interests; the structure of partnership; de Gaulle against it

EVER since the war, America has given unwavering support for European unity. The Atlantic alliance has provided a shield for Western Europe behind which the Communities could be built. Marshall Aid enabled Europe's economy to revive. Strongly influenced by Monnet, successive American administrations have consistently encouraged and pressed for the construction of the Communities. This policy was naturally believed by the Americans to be in their own interests, but in scope and style it transcended all the norms of foreign policy in the past: it was more the act of men who had caught the tide of history than the transactions of conventional diplomacy.

Europe has eagerly accepted American support. The European statesmen have quite well understood that Western Europe without America would long since have fallen subject to a Russian hegemony. This was itself the strongest motive for the American policy: Russia, with the control of Europe's great industrial potential, would before long have surpassed America in economic and military power. America and Europe also have strong economic interests in common. Their trade and their currencies closely interact, and the weakness of one is bad for the other. They have mutual interest in a stable and healthy world economy, and between them they have much of the power to make it so.

After Monnet's Europe had been irreversibly launched, which it was believed would be the case on Britain's accession to the Community, the next phase of Monnet's revolution would have consolidated this collaboration between Europe and America in an Atlantic partnership. It was explained in chapter 2 how a Community of nations should be based on a balance in which at least its two or three largest members are of similar size, thus eschewing the domination of the group by one nation which is much more powerful than the others. The same principle led Monnet to believe that the relationship between America and Europe should be that between two pillars—the United States and the European Community —supporting the Atlantic arch, rather than between American giant and European dwarfs. A partnership between two such pillars would be of a democratic character, contrasting with the more imperialistic concept of a hegemony. Co-operation between two partners with powerful interests in common would also be much more effective than it could be between a number of nations in an inter-governmental organisation such as the OEEC, particularly if the partnership were enshrined in substantial long-term commitments.

A hegemony is inevitably less agreeable for the European peoples than such a partnership. It is also for practical reasons less desirable. For, as the history of the Trade Expansion Act has shown, America makes concessions that are necessary for the good of her relations with Europe when the strength of an effective European Community forces her to reconsider her policies; and a similar reasoning applies to the obtaining by Europe of a share in the formation of policies about the nuclear deterrent. This is occurring as Europe's strength revives, and the European nations combined in a European Defence Community would have correspondingly greater influence. In Europe equally the response to the needs of the times is likely to be inadequate so long as the European nations, divided and therefore impotent, rely too heavily on American responsibility and initiative. This is seen in the feebleness of Europe's efforts to provide the developing countries with enough economic aid or itself with adequate conventional defence, although this would reduce the possibility of a disastrous nuclear war. Europe, feeling that the burden of solving these problems rested primarily with America, has failed to do what it should have done. But Europe's full support is essential if strategic and economic needs are to be met; and now that Europe's economy is strong and prosperous, American resentment at Europe's short-sighted meanness could boil over and subside into isolationism, unless Europe begins to pull its weight; and this is unlikely to happen unless the European peoples are so solidly combined that they feel strong enough to play a part comparable to that of America.

For these reasons, a partnership between equals was agreed by both the Europeans and the American administration to be the best form of collaboration for the future. On British accession to the Community, the time would have been ripe for this new venture. Europe's united strength was becoming great enough to make it possible; this same strength would, by altering the power relationship between America and Europe, inevitably create tensions that would be properly eased only by a new effort to make co-operation still closer than in the past; and many problems of deep concern to both partners—in defence, the stability of the world economy and the insistent demand of the emergent countries for help in speeding their economic growth—were urgently crying out to be solved. Ways were therefore being sought, to which the Trade Expansion Act was a signpost, to make the relationship between America and Europe more intimate and more organic.

In the political philosophies of de Gaulle and of Monnet, which start from opposite poles and clash head-on at almost every point of contact, there is no conflict more violent than that in attitudes and policies towards America. The policy of partnership is anathema to de Gaulle. Though reason must tell him that the support of America is needed so long as the European nations cannot match the nuclear armoury of Russia, his hatred of America appears to be so deep that he is willing to strike attitudes and pursue policies that could drive the Americans into isolationism. Whether these are rationalised in his mind as intended merely to insert himself between America and the rest of the Continent as leader of the latter in alliance with America, at least for the years which France would require in such circumstances to catch up in nuclear capability, or whether he conceives them as a legitimate brinkmanship designed to reduce, though not eliminate, the links across the Atlantic, is not likely to be so very important. His instinctive hostility is liable to make the style and reach of his actions irrationally provocative and dangerous to the alliance; and his ignorance of economic considerations, combined with his strong obstructive position as ruler of a key member of the

Economic Community, will probably result in renewed attempts to disrupt the still far from adequate organisation of the free world economy.

American policies towards Europe: multilateral force, Trade Expansion Act; no isolation, no capitulation, no domination

De Gaulle has now made his bid to exclude American and British influence from Europe and at the same time to dominate the Five. It was concluded in chapter 5 that America's great strength can be of major help to the Five in their efforts to stand up to him and resist a French hegemony.

America can provide this help by keeping open the offer of partnership and, until Monnet's Europe is relaunched and the European pillar is therefore available, by means of practical co-operation with the European nations, and especially the Five, in a manner that clearly points the way to future partnership.

The basis of this policy should be similar to American policy in the past: to use American military and economic power so as to serve the common interests of America and Europe. It should be done in such a way as to show the Five clearly that de Gaulle can offer them no comparable benefits.

The idea of the multilateral force is a good example of this line of thought. De Gaulle claims that he will eventually be able to offer Europe some nuclear protection. America in fact provides a massive protection. Its durability can be made more certain if European nations take part in providing it. If they do this as part of a multilateral force from which they do not have national contingents to withdraw, there is a strong presumption that they will not, at some stage, defect from the Atlantic alliance in order to follow de Gaulle. De Gaulle's ambition of hegemony is therefore stymied and at the same time a foundation has been laid for the relaunching of Monnet's Europe; for a multilateral force, when either France or Britain or both participate in it fully together with the Five, could be the cornerstone of a European Defence Community.

The Trade Expansion Act was the economic arm of partnership and although, with de Gaulle obstructing from inside the Community, the results will probably be a shadow of the original hopes, it is essential for America to persist in the tariff negotiations in order that the Five shall not feel that her great economic weight has been neutralised or even turned against them.

The Americans must, indeed, resist any impulse to retreat into isolation. It has already been shown earlier that reason urges them not to do so. Walter Lippman has, indeed, suggested that de Gaulle provokes America only because he knows that American protection will not in fact be withdrawn. But the springs of de Gaulle's actions are not so rational as Mr. Lippman seems to believe, and for America's part Dean Acheson has asserted that continued American collaboration cannot be taken totally for granted.

With the weakness of their balance of payments, the Americans are forced to try to check the outflow of dollars, and one way is to reduce military spending abroad. Some Americans are strongly advocating that they should cut their commitments in Europe. If de Gaulle succeeds in sabotaging the tariff negotiations, and especially if France's agricultural protectionism combines with Germany's immobilism in agricultural policy, so that the Community rigidly rejects any concessions to maintain the Community's imports of agricultural produce from America, the dollar's troubles will be intensified. Americans will at the same time feel a natural revulsion against Europe's narrow selfishness following on American postwar generosity, and the temptation to save the dollar by pulling out of Europe will be strong. Dangerous currents of opinion could flow more swiftly on both sides of the Atlantic, exacerbating one another with cumulative effect, and the result might be a doubtless irrational but certainly understandable withdrawal of America into its shell, just as occurred after the demoralising antics of European statesmen at the Peace Conference in 1919. But it is quite essential that Americans should keep any such emotions under control. The abandonment of Europe to de Gaulle and perhaps eventually to Russia would be incalculably dangerous.

The Americans should at the same time be determined not to capitulate to de Gaulle. They should fight hard at the tariff negotiations; French diplomacy has been supremely skilful at seeking out and using the points of identity between the interests of the Five and France. America should likewise incessantly emphasise the points where her interests coincide with those of the Five, and persistently press home her advantage.

Above all, America should not capitulate by giving de Gaulle the Bomb on his own terms, or indeed on any other terms. He has demonstrated that "collaborate with the West and the East, where necessary contract alliances with one side or the other" is probably a serious statement of intention. It would be madness for America to give these weapons to somebody who may well intend to contract an alliance with the other side.

Finally, the Americans should resist any temptation to abandon the doctrine of partnership and to try instead to perpetuate a hegemony over Europe. It is quite legitimate for America to apply diplomatic pressure on the Continentals and on Britain to encourage them to resist de Gaulle and to work for the relaunching of Monnet's Europe; and America's close alliance with and strong influence over Germany is particularly valuable in this regard. But American pressure on the nations of Europe has never crossed the bounds of decency and wisdom; for example, when the British foolishly resisted the supranational character that the Americans and some of the Continental countries, notably France, wanted to give the OEEC when it was established, the Americans did not insist. It would be a pity if America were to lose patience and to cease to respect its European allies in this way, and tragic if the difficulties in Europe caused the Americans to conclude that partnership was a pipe-dream and the domination of their awkward friends in Europe the only practical policy.

Patient, persistent support for Monnet's Europe

The task for America, then, is to maintain the trend of its previous policies in Europe: not to be stampeded by de Gaulle into isolation, capitulation or attempts to impose a permanent hegemony over Europe: but to continue to support the ideas of Monnet's Europe and of its partnership with America.

American reactions since the veto and the rebuff to their offer of nuclear help to de Gaulle have corresponded to these principles. The multilateral force has been proposed which, as explained above, could seal off the rest of the Continent from de Gaulle's strategic ambitions and later help in the relaunching of Monnet's Europe; and the purposes of the Trade Expansion Act have been tenaciously pursued in the tariff negotiations at Geneva.

But if the Americans are to support the Europeans until the battle against de Gaulle has been won, they must be patient and persistent even if their efforts are rewarded mainly by disappointments and provocations for a number of years.

7

BRITAIN'S CHOICE

IN 1945 Britain's reputation throughout Europe was immense. So when the Europeans decided to construct Europe anew on lines that would make internecine war impossible, they naturally sought leadership from Britain. But the British, preoccupied with welfare reforms at home and the dissolution of the empire overseas, and above all unaware that a radical change was needed in the international system based on the absolute power of the nation-state, remained coldly aloof from the Europeans' ideas.

France, like Britain, has a heritage of national grandeur that makes a supranational or federal system hard for many Frenchmen to swallow. Nevertheless, with their confidence in the national state eroded by the shocks of war, enough of them accepted the idea of Monnet's Europe for France to be able to play the leading role in the establishment of the three Communities.

Just when the British, seeing the Communities an established fact and at the same time experiencing the difficulties of a middle-sized nation on its own, were moving towards acceptance of the principles of Monnet's Europe, de Gaulle took command in France and ordered French policy to turn about. With gaullist France against Monnet's Europe and Britain excluded by the veto, the Europeans and the Five can make no progress. For Europe needs at least one or other of these prima donnas if the show is to go on.

Britain, if it adopted the building of Monnet's Europe as a major objective, could therefore play a central part in relaunching the whole conception. This would certainly be the only quick way to get it moving again, and as long as the French government is against the Community idea, it will remain the only way. There could be no more effective pressure on the French government and people to mend their ways and return to the fold of Monnet's Europe, than the

prospect that European leadership might otherwise pass to
Britain. But unlike the United States, which the last chapter
suggested should stick tenaciously to its existing policies,
Britain must make a decisive and radical choice if it is to
resist the challenge of de Gaulle and help to direct Europe
once more on to a constructive path.

Britain's choice: defensive sovereignty or pragmatic federalism

What precisely is the choice that Britain must make? The
essence of the case presented by de Gaulle at his press conference, shorn of its more lurid misconceptions and half-truths,
was that "the nature, structure and economic context of
England differ profoundly from those of the other States of
the Continent" and that Britain could qualify as a member
only by "transforming itself enough to belong to the Community without restriction and without reservation, and
placing it ahead of anything else". Britain's choice would be
first to transform its "nature, structure and economic context", and then to take what sounded remarkably like a vow
of marriage with the Continent.

But analysis shows that, in fact, there are wide differences
among the Six in economic levels and structures; that in
a surprising number of features, such as tariff levels, wages,
the proportion of national income spent by the government or
the proportions of direct and indirect taxation, Britain is near
the average of the Six; and that, moreover, the economic
structure of Western Germany and the part it plays in world
trade are much more akin to those of Britain than to those of
France. As for the marriage vow, the British government had
agreed to take this in respect to the economic matters encom-
passed by the three Communities, and Monnet, who in contrast to de Gaulle has some right to speak as their guardian,
has proclaimed his belief that Britain as a member would have
"consolidated her own European evolution and reinforced
ours".[1]

It is not to be supposed, however, that de Gaulle's half-
baked economic arguments were the heart of the matter. De
Gaulle is interested not in economics but in military power,
and his concern was not with tariffs, nor with the Economic
Community, nor even with the French peasant, but with the

---

[1] Interview with Jean Monnet, published in the *Corriere della Sera*,
7 April 1963.

British bomb. It is widely believed that, had Macmillan agreed to turn away from America and put Britain's nuclear capacity at the disposal of the French state, de Gaulle's veto would have been withdrawn. If this was so, then Britain's choice, summarised in de Gaulle's press conference as that of placing the Community "ahead of anything else", would have been to put her bomb at the disposal of himself, substituting a nuclear alliance with France for that with America. Macmillan would not agree to jeopardise the Western alliance and the veto fell.

That nuclear price could not be paid. Nor is there any other bribe with which Britain could buy its way past the gaullist veto. Thus Britain's choice cannot be aimed at placating de Gaulle. On the contrary, her only real alternative to passivity while de Gaulle fights it out with the democrats and Europeans on the Continent is to give the latter her unqualified support.

This means to accept the full implications of Monnet's Europe: that major political decisions in defence and economics will eventually be taken in common with other nations by a system centred on the majority vote; and that such a system must be based upon Europe because this is where a balanced group of peoples, ready to join together their sovereignty in this way, can be found. One must be quite clear that this is a full political commitment: although the national governments play a big part in framing decisions by the Community method—indeed in the existing Economic Community it is only the governments acting collectively in the Council of Ministers that can take the major decisions—no one government can act unilaterally on certain vital matters: there is a transfer of the seat of power where sovereignty is exercised on behalf of the people: the hard shell of the nation-state is eroded by a process of pragmatic federalism.

This is the political commitment which underlay the creation of the three Communities; which still underlies the aspirations of the Five; and which has been abandoned by de Gaulle. It has been argued that only if Britain is ready to accept this commitment can the Five successfully play poker with de Gaulle in the Economic Community; for only then will his ace, the threat of withdrawal, be bettered by the fair certainty that the Community would be solidly rebuilt with Britain in place of France. Only if Britain accepts this commitment, moreover, could Monnet's Europe be relaunched by means of a Defence Community. But in either case, Britain's conversion to Monnet's Europe would have to be explicit and unequivocal: completely credible to the Europeans on the Continent as well as the basis for determined action by the British.

To make such a commitment is a radical and probably irrevocable step. Should Britain take it?

It has already been explained why Monnet's Europe and Monnet's revolution are the most hopeful means of assuring peace and prosperity in Europe and of bringing progress towards a more orderly world. The evil effects that de Gaulle's veto could have on Britain if she were permanently excluded or if the Community broke up were described in chapter 1. To Britain, on the doorstep of Europe, the fate of the Continent is more important than ever before. 1940 is two decades ago and the Channel no longer a defensive moat. Western Europe's industries, forming a complex second only to that of America, represent immense power to do good or ill, and to none more than to a nation only twenty miles away. Excluded from this complex, Britain will have comparatively little power to do what it seeks to do in the world, whether this is to help the developing countries, to influence the defence policies of America, or to encourage a disarmament agreement with Russia. Nor will Europe, so long as its progress is checked by de Gaulle, do much to help solve the vital world problems such as hunger, poverty, economic development and the Bomb; indeed, if Europe became set in a gaullist mould it would be a menace to anyone trying to solve these problems. Since their solution is essential to the people of Britain's crowded island, this is for the British one of the most lamentable consequences of de Gaulle, and one of the most pressing reasons for a full British participation in the relaunching of Monnet's Europe.

Acceptance of such arguments has been undermined in Britain by a number of fallacies. Prominent among them is a supposition that, if economic problems are tackled, political problems can be left to look after themselves. There is some danger that the current version of this would be a European policy directed merely at satisfying Britain's economic interests, whether by eventual entry into the Community, or a form of association with it, or a degree of tariff cutting in GATT, or

some kind of free trade area if the Community is destroyed by
de Gaulle. But such a policy would be unlikely to succeed even
in its limited objectives because unless gaullism is repulsed
there is no place for Britain in the Community. Even if de
Gaulle's behaviour is intolerable the Community is more likely
to bog down as a half-made customs union, whose external
tariff is hard to reduce, than to fall apart and make way for a
free trade area. And even if, despite these difficulties, Britain's
economic interests were satisfied for a time, this would still
leave completely unresolved the fundamental political issue of
the nation-state and its inability to deal with the vast problems
of the modern world: the very issue that the Communities
were established to confront.

A second British fallacy is that the political issue is a straight
fight between liberals on the one side and illiberals on the
other. If this were so, Britain would be the victor and de
Gaulle the vanquished today, because the governments of the
Five are far closer to Britain's generally liberal view of the
world than to de Gaulle's. But there is not just one dichotomy:
liberal versus illiberal. There is another: federalist versus
nationalist, the federalists accepting the political implications
of Monnet's Europe and the nationalists opposing them. There
are therefore four main groups: *illiberal and nationalist*, personified by de Gaulle; *illiberal and federalist*, represented by a
certain right-wing segment of Continentals who are susceptible
to gaullism but who nevertheless support the Community institutions; *liberal and federalist*, that is to say the Europeans
and, on the whole, the governments of the Five; and *liberal
and nationalist*—the British, the Scandinavians and the Swiss.
Of course, the lines are not so sharply drawn as this, and there
has been movement between the groups, in particular the
British movement towards the federalist concepts of the Communities in the last three years. But so long as the liberal
elements, which include the Europeans and the governments
of Britain and the Five, are split into federalist and nationalist
wings, or suspect that they are so split, de Gaulle can drive a
wedge between them so that the liberals cannot fight
effectively.

The drawbacks of the nationalist system of inter-governmental co-operation, when compared with the Community
method of taking decisions in common, were analysed in
chapter 2. It is possible that de Gaulle, by posing the issues

very clearly, will have shown that the two dichotomies are in fact one dichotomy : liberals cannot remain nationalist because insistence on absolute national sovereignty is incompatible with a liberal view of the world. The British in particular, with their pragmatic political tradition that sets out to compose the interests of the different groups involved in a political issue rather than to impose the will of one man or group upon the rest, should see that this can be done effectively only within institutions that enable the groups, as the Community institutions do, to consider their interests together before coming to a decision—clear and consistent decisions being essential, and possible to reach only by the domination of one power or by using the technique of the majority vote.

There is also the practical consideration that the Europeans and the Five believe strongly in the Community method as well as in the liberal attitude, and that British initiatives in Europe will therefore be doomed to failure unless they are based on the Community method.

Another illusion that must be scotched is the assumption that what happens on the Continent is not of great concern to Britain because, in the last resort, the British can solve their own problems alone and carry great influence in dealing with the world's ills in general. With a century of world domination only recently behind them, this attitude of the British may be understandable but for a nation of Britain's size in a world of giants it is just not practical. Closely bound up with it is the belief that the Commonwealth gives Britain a power and influence far beyond that of other European nations of similar size.

But the Commonwealth now adds virtually nothing to Britain's power and little to its influence. Australia, Canada and New Zealand would certainly be likely to stand side by side with Britain in any grave crisis, but in doing so they would be aligned with the Atlantic alliance rather than with Britain alone. They will not contemplate any merging of sovereignty with Britain such as would ensure in normal times a common policy and hence an access of power and influence, for the understandable reason that Britain, being more powerful, would dominate them. Less understandably, Australia and New Zealand do not seem willing to consider Community or federal solutions on a wider scale, in which the British would be balanced by other nations of similar size. The solution to

their problems, therefore, is to be found in the context of an
Atlantic partnership, as proposed in chapter 11.

The other members of the Commonwealth are emergent
nations which may value the political consultations, but which
quite properly set store mainly by the practical benefits they
get from the Commonwealth, that is to say largely from
Britain, in terms of economic and educational advantages. If
they get more such benefits from other countries, the Commonwealth has no magic that will give it precedence when
they make their foreign policy decisions. If they get more from
America and the Continent than from Britain, then America
and the Continent will come first in their thinking. The contacts and the ease of communication between the British and
the overseas Commonwealth that have resulted from connections over many years and from a common educational background and the use of the English language are very valuable
and undoubtedly increase the effectiveness of British dealings
with those countries. But America and the Continent together
have seven times Britain's population and about ten times its
economic weight, and any attempt by Britain to exercise great
power or influence through its special relationship with the
emergent Commonwealth countries and in competition with
America and the Economic Community is consequently almost bound to fail.

The only rational policy for Britain, then, is to join its forces
with those of other advanced countries in promoting the development of emergent nations, as is proposed in chapter 12.
The British will carry more weight if they exert influence on
the policies of the European Community and the Atlantic
partnership than if they try to act independently with their
comparatively slender resources. Within this context, Britain's
connections with Commonwealth countries and understanding
of their problems can be a priceless asset.

If the policies of the European Community were irremedi-
ably prejudicial to the interests of the emergent nations, then
membership would be the wrong policy for Britain. The suggestion has been made, typified in the term "tight, inward-
looking", that an organisation such as the Community with
common institutions designed to form effective common policies is necessarily going to be illiberal. The probability is in
fact the opposite. Where national decisions are taken, or where
the need for unanimity inserts an undiluted national element

into the taking of collective decisions, then national phobias are compounded. This would clearly be the case in a loose European coalition such as de Gaulle proposes. But when common decisions are taken by procedures that involve the use or the possibility of a majority vote, prejudices of this sort fade into the background. A European Political Community would have been more reasonable than the French about Algeria or than the British about Cyprus, because these policies were based on national passions that were shared by none of the other members. The concentration of the Economic Community's collective aid and of its preferential favours on the colonies and ex-colonies of its members was due solely to the need to have French agreement to establish the Community at all, *i.e.* on the power that France had to veto its establishment if French demands of this sort were not met. The system of association would never have had its excessively nationalist slant if it had been decided upon by a majority vote. It would in fact be more accurate to use the terms "tight, outward-looking" and "loose, inward-looking" than the opposite clichés that have been a part of the mythology of anti-Community elements in Britain.

It is, however, true that a gaullist Community would almost certainly pursue policies that would damage outsiders, whether the white Dominions and other Western countries or the emergent nations apart from the Community's associates. Such a Community would likewise hold small comfort for those who believe in democratic methods of government. The emergence of rampant gaullism, authoritarian and nationalist, does at least bring with it the advantage of an open conflict with the forces of liberalism and democracy, whose result will be stamped clearly on the Community's character and policies. If de Gaulle won, it would be a Community that Britain would not be allowed to join and should not wish to join, if indeed it remained a Community at all. If the Europeans win, then it will be a Community open to Britain and with similar basic aims and interests.

Thus the interests of the British coincide with those of the Europeans. Britain should give them her full support during their struggle with de Gaulle and be clearly available to join with them in building the European Community as soon as there is an opportunity to do so. Will the British choose to do so, in the knowledge that they must be ready to accept the

Community method in the fields of foreign policy and defence as well as of economics? The answer cannot yet be given, but the possibilities can be indicated by examining the attitudes of the main political forces in Britain.

Reservations of Conservatives, Labour and the general public; if informed opinion leads the rest will follow

Britain's peacetime record in Europe is bad. In the 'thirties both governments and the public were blind and weak; in the 'fifties they were unimaginative, muddled and aloof. Their mixture of equivocation and outright hostility towards the Communities engendered Continental suspicions about Britain's intentions in her dealings with the Communities that are not yet dispelled. Much progress has been made since the application for membership in 1961, but the British have still to make a firm political commitment and to make it explicitly enough to remove any doubts from the Europeans' minds. Britain would, as Monnet has said, have become as Community-minded as the Six by experiencing, as a member, the Community method. Now she has the harder task of making the transition from a nation-centric to a Community point of view by a conscious effort of thought and will.

The Conservative Party and Government have made encouraging, indeed astonishing progress in the last three years. The application to join was clearly a milestone. The Cabinet includes such genuine proponents of the Community as Heath and Thorneycroft; the Party has its European wing and the Party Conference in 1962 was overwhelmingly in favour of membership.

Against this, there is the Conservatives' anti-Community wing, with the Beaverbrook press as its spokesman. If de Gaulle were British, this would be his political home. Whether the subject is the United Nations, the European Community, national sovereignty or attitudes to the "Empire", Beaverbrook and his friends can be relied upon to hold the opposite of the sensible view. They part company with de Gaulle, however, where his chauvinism is tempered with realism, as in his granting of independence to the colonies and to Algeria and his recognition of the need for a genuine alliance with Germany. This group is about as numerous in Parliament as are the Party's enthusiastic pro-Europeans, but there is virtually no prospect of its views making any headway.

The real weakness in the Conservative attitude has been reserve or equivocation about the political commitment. Macmillan said in August 1961, when he first explained to the House of Commons Britain's application for membership, that a federal solution was unacceptable and that the only practical solution would be a confederation, "a Commonwealth if you like". This ignored the fact that the Economic Community which he was applying to join is a federal, not a "Commonwealth" solution for economic affairs; and it unwisely and unnecessarily challenged the deep convictions of the Europeans who, as later events abundantly proved, are Britain's natural allies on the Continent.

This confusion of thought and irritation of the most sensitive spot in Community thinking were shown again by Macmillan in 1962. "The form which the political unity of the Community should take is now under active discussion in Europe, where opinions on it are strongly divided. There is a school which ardently believes in the unitary concept of a European Federation, a New European State. Here in Britain the Liberal Party Assembly voiced some strong support for this solution. I myself believe that the bulk of public opinion in this country, and certainly any Conservative Government, is firmly against the extinction of separate national identities and would choose a Europe which preserved and harmonised all that is best in our different national traditions. We would, I think, favour a more gradual approach worked out by experience, instead of a leap in the dark, and this is a view shared by many leaders of opinion in Europe."[1]

This is an understatement. There is practically no leader of opinion in Europe who wants to make a leap in the dark and to extinguish separate national identities. The pragmatic Community approach is generally approved. But to launch an attack on the federal method which underlies the Community approach serves only to exacerbate the suspicions of supporters of the Community. What they need instead is an assurance that the British are willing to apply the Community method to political as well as economic unity. Had they been given this, the result of de Gaulle's veto might have been very different; and whether or not they get such an assurance will

[1] Harold Macmillan, *Britain, the Commonwealth and Europe,* the Conservative and Unionist Central Office, 1962.

probably determine the future prospects for British participation in the Community.

Macmillan deserves great credit for having brought the Conservative Party and the country to the brink of membership of the Economic Community. It is not his fault that de Gaulle chose to cast the veto. This was a risk that had to be taken. But to equivocate about the political commitment was a serious mistake that must not be repeated. Macmillan doubtless made it partly because he was not clear in his mind about the meaning of the Community method and of the alternative of coalition diplomacy. But he also steered clear of the political commitment in response to forces in his own Party which reject the political implications of the Community method, and which were reflected as much in the over-hasty conclusion of the Nassau agreement without consultation with Britain's prospective partners in the European Community, as in the fuzzy statements on the subject of political unity.

These basically anti-Community forces must be confronted and overcome if the Conservatives are to play their full part in bringing Britain into the Community. There are grounds to believe that centre opinion in the parliamentary Party was well aware that Community treatment would eventually be applied to political as well as economic matters, but did not wish to admit it openly because they were afraid of public opinion. It is therefore reasonable to suppose that the majority of Conservatives will come to accept the idea of a Political Community if they think that it will be acceptable to the public.

After the war the Labour Government missed a historic opportunity. All Europe looked to Britain for an initiative towards the building of a new Europe but, as M. Spaak said, "alas, we looked in vain".[1] The Conservatives were loud in criticism but their own performance in their first years of office showed that as far as insularity went there was little to choose between the two parties. In recent years, however, the Labour Party has not made the same progress as the Conservatives.

The contrast was seen in sharpest relief at the Party Conferences in 1962. While the Conservatives lined up solidly behind the policy of entry into the Community, the Labour

---

[1] Anthony Nutting, *Europe will not wait*, Hollis & Carter, 1960, p. 3.

Party adopted a much more critical attitude than the mere logic of opposition might have demanded.

The policy agreed at the Brighton Conference was not entirely negative. Entry into the Community was accepted if five main conditions were fulfilled. Three of these were themselves reasonable enough : fair conditions to be negotiated for the Commonwealth, British agriculture and the EFTA countries. Two of the conditions, however, showed a prejudice against the principles of solidarity and common action on which the Community is based. The demand for an independent foreign policy was not formally incompatible with membership of the Economic Community, although it was in complete contrast to the concept of Monnet's Europe and the point of view of the Europeans, and it is hard to see in logic why common action should be acceptable for tariffs and all questions relating to foreign trade but anathema in respect of other aspects of foreign policy. Nor was insistence on independent planning entirely contrary to the Rome Treaty, although Article 103 states that "member-states shall consider their policy relating to economic trends as a matter of common interest". Dr. Erhard, who is a doctrinaire anti-planner, has been fighting against the European Commission's proposals for co-ordinating national plans at the Community level. But, for a Party that believes in long-term planning as the necessary basis for economic policy to agree to enter a Common Market provided that national plans are not co-ordinated is practically incomprehensible. If economic planning is necessary and economic barriers between nations are removed, then the plans for the whole Common Market must clearly be made compatible with each other, at least as far as the assumptions regarding the flow of trade, workers and capital between the members are concerned.

The failure of logic in the Labour Party's position was the product of a dichotomy within the Party. On the one side there was the European wing and the general reluctance to come down formally against a new venture in international co-operation. On the other there was a suspicion, which had been intensified by the development of the de Gaulle-Adenauer axis and Belgian reactions to the Congo crisis, that the Community was dominated by reactionaries who would exploit the workers within it and the developing countries without. Unfortunately, it seemed too that such suspicions were still coloured by an unpleasant prejudice against foreigners on the other side of the Channel.

Yet the prospects for the development of a healthier and more progressive attitude in the Labour Party are not altogether gloomy. If there is a Labour government, the responsibility of office may bring home both the foolishness of eschewing involvement in Continental affairs, thus increasing the danger of a Continent dominated by de Gaulle, and the harsh economic outlook for a Britain excluded from the big trading groups. Mr. Wilson, without the millstone of an independent deterrent round his neck, would find less difficulty than the Conservatives in participating in a multilateral force, which can be one step towards an integrated Europe in an Atlantic partnership. Admittedly he said soon after the Brussels breakdown : "We shall make more progress, whether in economic or political co-operation, the less we aim at federal or supranational solutions, the more we work within an inter-governmental framework."[1] But this need not be accepted as a statement of rooted and considered principle. Mr. Wilson cannot surely fail to see that the record of the Communities between 1958 and 1962 shows progress unparalleled by that of any inter-governmental organisation, and that this progress has been retarded only by the nationalistic use of the typically inter-governmental weapon of the veto. He appears, indeed, to have an open mind on the subject and would be likely to take up a position where he senses the centre of Labour Party opinion to be.

The Parliamentary Party has a vigorous European wing about as large as the European wing of the Conservatives. Like the Conservatives, it also has its diehard anti-Europeans. The views of the much larger group in the centre who are essentially "don't knows" will be greatly influenced by the progress of the Social Democrat parties on the Continent, towards whom the Labour Party has often shown an unfortunately condescending attitude. Germany is particularly important. The replacement of Adenauer by Erhard will already be a step in the right direction as far as the Labour Party is concerned; a further strengthening of the German Social Democrats between now and the 1965 elections would be still better.

[1] Speech by Harold Wilson in the House of Commons, 11 February 1963.

It is also reasonable to hope that, if the Labour Party gains power, it will take a more realistic view of the social and economic progress made by the Communities and of the need for international planning as canvassed by the European Commission.

Thus, if there is a Labour government, the Party should develop a more positive European policy, particularly if the Social Democrat forces on the Continent are becoming stronger; and it is by no means impossible that, if opinion in the country as a whole is not unfavourable, the Party would, like its counterparts on the Continent, come to support the principles of Monnet's Europe.

Neither of the two main parties, then, has its mind closed for or against the Community, and the policies of both will depend on the drift of opinion in the country.

Towards the end of the Brussels negotiations, the Gallup polls showed as many people against British entry as in favour. But the atmosphere was one of uncertainty, with an equal number again who were undecided, rather than of hostility. People felt that they had not had time to adjust to the idea of a great change, with political implications which they did not understand and which the government had done little to clarify. Since the negotiations broke down there has not been a reaction against Europe. Indeed, a Gallup poll held soon after de Gaulle's press conference showed that almost half the public favoured membership, compared with around a third in previous weeks. The general public, like the average member of the Conservative or Labour Parties, remains open to persuasion on the subject.

In these circumstances, everything depends on the evolution of those sectors of opinion that provided the hard core of the support for British entry into the Economic Community: almost the whole of the press apart from the Beaverbrook newspapers and the *Daily Worker* and eventually the *Guardian*; the progressive elements in industry, which included most of the larger firms; most people in the relevant Ministries in Whitehall; most of the younger people in Parliament; the Liberal Party; and the European wings of Labour and of the Conservatives.

It might have been expected that these groups would be disillusioned by the veto. In fact their line has become if anything more positive. *The Economist*, which led the movement

of opinion in favour of membership of the Economic Community, has come out in favour of integration in defence
arrangements, with the clear implication of Political Community. Other papers and journals have maintained their
position in respect of British participation in economic integration. And the lines taken by the papers seem to reflect the
attitudes of the sectors of opinion mentioned above. Thus Lord
Gladwyn has called for a supranational Political Authority
acting, after a transitional period, by majority vote; and the
bulk of the support for British membership of the Community
remains.

Thus since the veto the prospects that substantial sectors of
British opinion will come to accept the idea of a Political
Community have improved. Any such movement of opinion is
valuable because it increases the Continentals' estimation of
Britain's availability as a positive factor in Monnet's Europe,
and hence their ability to resist gaullist attempts at domination. But there is little hope of a satisfactory outcome for
Britain herself unless the ideas of Monnet's Europe are
accepted by the government and a good majority of the
public.

It is not yet possible to say whether the movement of
opinion will go so far; it can only be asserted that, with
opinions as they stand today, it is well within the realms of
possibility. A major change of policies and views would certainly still be required. The remains of a patronising attitude
towards the Continent would have to be swept away. Symp-
toms of insularity such as an instinctive hostility to the idea of
naval crews of mixed nationality would have to go. The
stubborn refusal of many people to accept the Germans as
allies on an equal footing, despite their sensible and reliable
behaviour in the last fifteen years, would have to be repudiated. The comfortable fuzziness in Britain's view of the world
would have to be replaced by a sharper awareness of Britain's
place in relation to that of other countries. A more positive
outlook would have to be adopted in place of the refusal to
take initiatives and the carping reaction to the initiatives of
others that have characterised so much of British policy since
the war.

The British people are, however, beginning to realise that
big changes in national habits and attitudes are required. If
they understand that Britain's part in world affairs is likely

to be meagre without participation in Monnet's Europe; that readiness to participate can be a considerable factor in preventing the emergence of a chauvinistic, gaullist Continent, and in bringing about a pacific Europe and a more orderly world; and that, having been five years too late in accepting European responsibilities in the 'thirties and in the recent past, it would be unforgivable to be five years too late once again, there is a strong possibility that they will accept the need for the radical change in Britain's view of the world that Monnet's Europe implies. To judge from Britain's postwar behaviour alone, such optimism could hardly be justified. But the historical record shows a sense of reality that has for many centuries enabled the British to understand and meet the changing conditions of the times. It may reasonably be hoped, and indeed expected, that they will do so once again.

PART III

TOWARDS A FEDERAL EUROPE

8

THE ECONOMIC COMMUNITY

A foundation for Monnet's Europe; progress blocked by de Gaulle; the need for Britain to be available

THE Europeans established the Economic Community as a foundation for Monnet's Europe. Believing that many of Europe's problems could be solved only by common action by the European peoples, they wanted institutions within which the member-countries would be irrevocably committed to work together, and which would be strong enough to banish for ever the fear of war between them. They understood that this required some powers to be removed from the exclusive control of the separate national governments and exercised jointly in the new institutions.

It was in the economic field that they persuaded their peoples to take this most radical step. For not only would a Community embracing the European economies be a clear move towards a new political system and away from the jealous nationalisms of the past; there was also the hope that a large market comparable to that of the United States would enable Europeans to secure something like the Americans' enviable prosperity. Thus material interest was grafted on to a political idea; the Economic Community, together with Euratom and their forerunner, the Coal and Steel Community, was the result. Power is being transferred to the Community in certain key sectors of economic policy, particularly in tariffs and agriculture. In this way the ills of economic nationalism are being eradicated and many of Europe's economic weaknesses overcome.

The Economic Community has sometimes been falsely classed as a technical body without political competence. De Gaulle constantly tries, by word and deed, to reduce it to that status. But as Professor Hallstein has rightly insisted, many of the Community's decisions are highly political acts. Changes in the level of tariffs and of agricultural prices are matters of great political consequence, affecting the incomes and employment of millions of people. In taking such decisions by majority vote, the Community institutions will be acting as a federal government in a certain limited field. It is not, as is so often assumed, just an economic prelude to federation; it is a federal system of a new form applied to a restricted sector of economic life.

It has been suggested that the Economic Community is only half complete: lacking sufficient powers in economic and monetary policy and needing a democratic reinforcement of its institutions. The European Commission, in its Action Programme published in 1962, proposed ways of overcoming many of these deficiencies by stronger procedures for forming economic and monetary policies, by co-ordinating economic planning, by an acceleration to bring forward the third stage of the transitional period when majority voting becomes more general, and by a whole series of decisions in different sectors of policy. The democratic strengthening of the Community has been demanded by the European Parliament, with its Draft Convention for instituting direct elections; while unofficial proposals have been made for giving the Parliament a greater share in the control of policy, at present the preserve of the national governments voting in the Council of Ministers.

If reforms such as these were made, the Economic Community would in fact become one half of a federation: its institutions would be a federal government with powers over economic questions that comprise half the stuff of modern politics. It would have been so strengthened as to be not just a foundation, but one of the two great pillars of Monnet's Europe. The other pillar, without which Monnet's Europe would remain incomplete, would be a Community for foreign policy and defence.

Until the armed forces of the member-countries become integrated in a Community defence force, the Economic Community will never be really secure; for, with physical power remaining in the national armies, an intransigent member-government can resist the Community's decisions and the Community has no means of enforcing the law. And if the armed forces are integrated in a Defence Community, it follows that all those aspects of foreign policy linked with defence must come within the scope of the Community method as well. Ten years ago the Europeans tried to set up a Defence Community and failed. More recently, in their conflict with de Gaulle about the form of a European "political union", the Five put forward what would have amounted to a Community system for dealing with matters of foreign policy, with some provision for majority voting after a transitional period of three years. Although both these attempts were defeated because the French government did not agree, they represented the natural course of progress of the Community idea. There can be little doubt that, if the Economic Community were to continue to develop, with member-governments that are favourable to its basic concepts, a Community for foreign policy and defence would be formed as the second pillar of European construction, and Monnet's Europe would then be complete.

It was explained in chapter 3 that Monnet's Europe is but part of Monnet's revolution, which is the transformation of international relations throughout the world by the gradual spreading of the Community method. Just as the Economic Community has been the foundation for Monnet's Europe, so it has been the generator for his revolution, inducing the British application for membership, the American offer of partnership (of which the Trade Expansion Act was a first instalment), and a number of proposals for dealing with questions of Commonwealth and world trade that have been referred to earlier. The creation of the Community exposed and intensified some of the existing problems of the world economy, and the reaction was to deal with them by institutions or procedures that had something of the stamp of the Community method.

Thus the Economic Community is half an economic federation which is itself one half of a political federation. It is also the beginnings of Monnet's revolution. So long as the member-governments of the Community shared its basically federalist philosophy, the whole design seemed destined to follow from the first act of creation. Starting with the Economic Community, the Europeans were travelling on a royal road towards federation in Europe and a better order in the affairs of the world at large.

When de Gaulle returned to power in France, the Europeans feared his well-known aversion to the Community method. But he honoured the recently ratified Treaty of Rome and, during the years of the Algerian struggle, he interfered little with its working. The Europeans grew confident that he would not dare to disturb the Community for fear of losing the alliance of the Five; that the Community process was too strong for him to disrupt; that the gaullist cat had been belled.

But de Gaulle had left the Community in peace only because he was preoccupied elsewhere. In January 1963, disdaining the Community's proper procedures and the policies and attitudes of his fellow members, he ruthlessly cut short the negotiations with Britain that had been the focus of the Community's energies for over a year. It became clear that he would not let his methods of personal rule and his chauvinistic ambitions be fettered by the Community method. He was not a belled cat but a bull in a china shop.

In the face of this challenge, the Europeans want to keep the Community as a going concern, because its downfall would be a great setback for Monnet's Europe and because they need it as a foundation for progress when de Gaulle is gone. They are therefore not likely to break the law of the Treaty nor, by adopting a completely negative and disruptive policy, to give de Gaulle an excuse to break it himself. It is to be hoped, on the other hand, that they will not be frightened by any gaullist threats into accepting policies of which they disapprove or into refraining from the use of their powers when the Treaty provides for a majority vote. But however wise and brave they may be, the Europeans can make no substantial progress towards Monnet's Europe within the context of the Six alone while de Gaulle is there to stop them. The development of the Economic Community as laid down in the Rome Treaty is valuable, both psychologically and actually, in the short run; moreover, after a number of years, many interests will have become so strongly vested in the existence of the big single market that the most powerful economic and political forces will be massively in favour of safeguarding it by the completion of Monnet's Europe, and against any policies, such as de Gaulle's, that threaten to disrupt it. But for the next few years the political and economic infrastructure of Monnet's Europe will still be too weak for this, and de Gaulle will be able to block all proposals to strengthen the Economic Community or to apply the Community method to the foreign policy and defence of the Six. For the time being the Economic Community, which depends for its vitality on the co-operation of all its members, is not a basis for further advance.

If this royal road is closed to the Six, it is also closed to Britain; the veto is the roadblock which there is no getting round. The arguments in favour of membership, considered in chapter 7, are as strong as ever they were, but membership of the Economic Community is now by itself an inadequate and even useless aim for British policy. For de Gaulle will use his veto as long as he can; and he will be able to do so until he is beaten in a battle about the future political structure of Europe and its posture in the world as a whole.

It is the Europeans and the Five, rather than the British, who are in the front line of this battle. But they can fight more stoutly if Britain is known to be available as a member of a reconstructed Community, should the struggle with de Gaulle cause the existing one to fall apart. The threat of a French walk-out will then lose most of its terror and the Five will be better able to take the initiative; while de Gaulle for his part is likely to be more circumspect if there is the prospect that the Five would link up with Britain should his own behaviour become intolerable. The British should not hope that their availability would quickly result in membership; the object is to change the balance of power in the conflict within the Community : to be a solvent to weaken the position of gaullism and thus create the political conditions under which Monnet's Europe can be revived and full British participation again become possible.

British availability: politically determined; economically viable; negotiating problems solved

It is important to be clear what Britain's availability means. It is not enough for Britain just to want to be a member. It is not even enough for the Continentals to believe that Britain would be a good member if she joined a strong and self-confident Community. They have to be sure that Britain would step in and help to reconstruct a Community that had been badly shaken and perhaps shattered by the battle with de Gaulle; that Britain would not try, in the process, to weaken the Community's institutions and reduce it to an amorphous free trade area, but would share their concern to build an effective organ of international democracy.

Britain's availability will be credible to the Europeans only if the British are politically determined to take part in the Community process; if they are economically strong enough to do so; and if the main problems of the past negotiations have already been solved or it is clear that they will be solved. If any one of these conditions is not fulfilled, the Europeans will find it hard to confront de Gaulle's brinkmanship, because they will not be sure enough that Britain provides a genuine alternative.

Half-heartedness or equivocation about the political issue would be fatal. In the minds of the Europeans, the Economic Community is but one aspect of Monnet's Europe. Unless the British show that they accept the change in the structure of political power that Monnet's Europe implies, the Europeans will continue to doubt that Britain would be a valuable member of a Community in trouble. It will certainly help if the British government shows its political will for eventual membership by taking internal economic measures that are clearly designed to prepare for it. But the real test will be the British attitude to the Community method in general: to a federal system for foreign policy and defence as well as economics.

The economic viability of Britain is almost as important. In 1958 there were doubts whether France, its economy ravaged by years of inflation, would in practice be able to accept even the first easy stages of the Community's transitional period. But under de Gaulle plans to restore order to the French economy were put into effect, and France was able to fulfil its obligations. There have likewise been some doubts as to whether Britain would be able to take the much deeper tariff cuts that would now be required on entry, without a balance-of-payments crisis followed by an escape from the rigours of the Treaty. If Britain's availability is to be sufficiently credible, such doubts must be put at rest.

In the short term, Britain's central economic need is to increase its exports fast. Modernisation and economic growth have been repeatedly checked by credit squeezes needed to save the pound, which exports themselves have been too sluggish to do. In Continental countries such as Germany and Italy, on the other hand, the surging expansion of exports has given a great impulse to the growth of the economy as a whole. Faster growth means more modern equipment and hence more competitive exports, so that Germany and Italy have been in a benign circle and Britain, conversely, in a vicious one.

Other objects of British economic policy should, therefore, be subordinated to the need to stimulate exports. The tax on added value, for example, which the members of the Economic Community are likely to adopt as their standard method of indirect taxation, allows a rebate which is an incentive to exporters, and objections of the Inland Revenue to this tax should therefore be over-ruled. Without directly subsidising exports, which would invite a new spiral of cut-throat economic nationalism, the government could give help for export research and promotion. If these and other similar measures fail to make exporting of sufficient interest to British businessmen, then it will be necessary to reduce the value of the pound to the point where they are moved to export enough.

The rapid expansion of exports is the immediate objective if faster growth of the British economy is to get firmly under way and if Britain is to look like a viable prospective member of Europe's trading community. In the longer run, it will be equally necessary to achieve a sustained growth-rate comparable to those that are normal on the Continent, say five per cent a year against Britain's postwar two-and-a-half per cent. For if Britain is outside the Economic Community for several years and growth-rates on either side of the Channel continue to diverge as in the past, Britain will again become an unconvincing applicant even if the immediate export problem has been overcome.

Two of the foundation stones of long-term economic growth have recently been laid in the form of the National Economic Development Council and an incomes policy. Growth depends on investment of the right quantity and quality, and French experience has shown how "indicative planning"—a combination of objective forecasting by the authorities with the help of industry and of gentle persuasion of the latter by the former—can help in achieving this. A policy to keep the rise of incomes within the rise of the value of production is equally necessary if growth is not to be distorted by inflation. Unfortunately the foundation stone of an incomes policy has been laid askew, for the National Incomes Commission has neither the support of organised labour nor any power to enforce its rulings.

The third great need, if Britain is to enjoy sustained growth, is a drive for better education for industry, from apprentices to top management. This is still gravely deficient in instilling into industry the requisite attitudes and skills.

Without these practical measures, a British intention to join the Economic Community will not be credible for long. Such measures would, indeed, be essential even if Britain had no thought of joining the Economic Community. But however successful they may be, they will not remove the basic economic arguments in favour of joining: the big market is increasingly necessary if there is to be room for modern large-scale enterprises to operate in competition with each other; and in the long run, the Community method is the only valid alternative to economic nationalism.

Even though Britain may be politically determined and economically viable, the Five will still have cause to doubt her status as a more or less automatic substitute for France if there are still formidable negotiating problems for which solutions have not been found. They would be less ready to take the risk that de Gaulle would remove himself from the Community, if it seemed that prolonged negotiations with the British might subsequently end in failure. From the British side, too, it is hard to envisage a government's reopening negotiations for membership unless it was virtually certain they would suceeed. It is therefore necessary to see how far the major problems can be solved in advance.

There are two fields in particular in which Britain should make unilateral moves towards the Continental system. It has been asserted above that in many ways Britain has a more typical European economy than any one of the Six; but in agriculture and taxation the British systems are out on a limb. Since in each case a move towards the Continental system would result in greater efficiency, it would have a threefold advantage: evidence of political will to remain available as a member; greater viability; and solution of difficult negotiating problems.

Apart from external questions concerning the relations of Britain and the Community with the outside world, the only real stumbling block encountered in the negotiations was the time that would have been allowed to bring British agriculture fully within the scope of the common agricultural policy. The British were hampered by the political difficulty of quickly reversing Britain's cheap food policy. But it is now time that this sacred cow of British politics was killed. In the nineteenth century and indeed up to recent years, cheap food was a vital element of national welfare, for a considerable proportion of the people had too little to eat and, had food been more expensive, would have had still less. This is, however, no longer so; as a nation the British probably eat too much. In limited sectors, such as old age pensioners, large families and the unemployed, the cupboard is still too bare; but the remedy for this is to pay these people more under the system of National Insurance and the welfare state. At present, instead, the whole nation's pattern of consumption is distorted in favour of food by tariffs and purchase taxes on manufactures and subsidies on home-produced foodstuffs. This is bad for the budget, bad for the balance of payments because so much of Britain's food is imported, bad for Britain's status as a potential member of the European Community and probably bad for the nation's health as well.

On the Continent, the wholesale prices of food are too high because inefficient local production is protected by tariffs averaging perhaps twenty per cent. It is to be hoped that the European Commission will succeed in its intention of getting these prices down, and the best policy for Britain would therefore be to go halfway towards the Community's present system : to impose a tariff of, say, ten per cent on imports of food and, since this would raise the wholesale prices of food on the British market, to cut farm subsidies correspondingly. The rise in revenue and fall in expenditure would give the government a wide margin to improve benefits for pensioners, large families and the unemployed, and to inject vigour into the economy by major tax cuts. In order to minimise any tendency for prices and wages to spiral, the new system could be introduced gradually over a period of years.

Taxation did not become an issue during the Brussels negotiations, partly because the Six were in such an early stage of considering the Community's own tax policy. Their current planning, however, favours various taxes that are more conducive to economic efficiency than those in Britain : the above-mentioned tax on added value; a single tax on incomes instead of two; a single tax on companies instead of two; a tax on capital; and a payroll tax. It would in any case be to Britain's advantage to adopt these systems of tax, and a potentially thorny problem of any future negotiation would at the same time be removed.

Although, apart from external questions, the recent negotiations exposed few obstacles in the way of including Britain in the Common Market and economic union, the Community, if its development is not frozen by de Gaulle, will be evolving common policies not only in agriculture and taxation but also in sectors such as transport, energy, cartels, labour and social questions. Obstacles could therefore arise if the policies of the Community and Britain diverge, and the gaullists will doubtless try to ensure that they do—de Gaulle's efforts to prevent regular consultations between Britain and the Six were evidence of that. But it is in the interests of both Britain and the Europeans to keep their policies as much in harmony as possible: for Britain, because this will help to secure her eventual entry into the Economic Community; for the Europeans, because Britain's credible availability is a powerful deterrent to intolerable acts on the part of de Gaulle and a safety-net in case the Community falls apart. The British have strengthened their Delegation to the Community and they should make it as strong as possible; continued good relations with the European Commission are one of the most important needs of British foreign policy. It has been agreed that Ministers of Britain and the Six are to meet quarterly. And the Anglo-German, Anglo-Italian and Anglo-Benelux Economic Committees can be used in order to maintain harmony between the policies of Britain and the Five.

If at any time a genuine offer of association were made, Britain should certainly accept it, provided that, after a transitional period, it was to lead to full membership. It might also be worth taking it up if it provided for Britain to have a real influence in the formation of Community policy, although it is hard in those circumstances to see what advantage this would have, from anybody's point of view, over full membership. But association with no influence over Community policies could hardly be acceptable, for the British would then be exposed to the full effects of decisions taken on the Continent in which they had no say: a sort of second class European citizenship in economic affairs.

The greatest need, however, if Britain is to be convincingly available as a potential member of the Economic Community, is for the external problems that dogged the Brussels negotiations to be solved, or at least clearly seen to be readily soluble. They may be classed into four groups of major importance: 1, imports of the products of temperate agriculture from the Commonwealth; 2, imports of industrial manufactures from EFTA; 3, imports of tropical products from Commonwealth countries in Asia, Africa and the West Indies; and 4, imports of manufactures from Commonwealth countries in Asia. It is possible that sterling would have become a major problem had the negotiations continued, and it is more than likely to be so in the future, especially if the Community develops a common monetary policy.

The solutions to some of these problems are to be found in tariff cuts by the Community and Britain. If the GATT negotiations following on the American Trade Expansion Act succeed, the position of advanced industrial countries outside the Community will be greatly eased. Not only would the common tariff bear less hardly on imports of manufactures from Canada and Australia and also, of course, from the United States, but any of the EFTA countries that did not wish to join the Community or agree to be associated with it on reasonable terms could find life tolerably comfortable outside. The Western markets for Indian cloth and other Asian manufactures could also be improved by tariff cuts as well as by agreements by the European countries to relax their import quotas progressively, on the lines of the Geneva agreement for cotton cloth but more generously drawn.

Commodity agreements were proposed during the Brussels negotiations to deal with the problems of temperate agriculture and are still agreed in principle to be the best way of organising this difficult sector of trade. It would not be easy for Britain, struggling with its own problems outside the Common Market, to agree to pay higher prices than at present, but she should be willing to pay her fair contribution if a commodity agreement includes a scheme for distributing such foodstuffs to developing countries. It has also been suggested that the earnings of developing countries from sales of tropical products should be stabilised by means of commodity agreements.

It was proposed during the Brussels negotiations that association should be offered to Commonwealth countries in Africa and comprehensive trade agreements negotiated to protect the exports of Commonwealth countries in Asia. Although

the offer of association is still open, the African countries have
not accepted it because they believe that some of the stigma
of colonial status attaches to it. This stigma, and the real
threat to the trade of Asian and Latin American countries
represented by the tariff preferences accorded under association, would be much less if the Six reduced their common
tariff on tropical products, which of course has no protective
element, to zero or nearly so. The difference between association and a comprehensive trade agreement could then be
comparatively slight, particularly if the comprehensive agreements provided for the supply of aid as does the agreement
on association.

It can hardly be expected that gaullist France would co-
operate in forming Community policies of this sort, which
would be both liberal and favourable to eventual British
membership. But to none of the techniques suggested does the
veto apply after the end of 1965. At that date, the Community's tariffs, quotas and other aspects of commercial policy
become subject to majority vote. Aid is not at present a Community matter nor does the Community provide for any veto
in questions of monetary policy, should international monetary
arrangements be proposed within which the problems of
sterling could be resolved. It would therefore be possible, if
the Europeans and the Five are convinced that it is the right
thing to do, to deal in spite of de Gaulle with many of these
external problems, particularly of Commonwealth trade,
which would otherwise loom up should new negotiations
between Britain and the Community be proposed.

It will be seen in chapters 11 and 12 that each of these
external problems, although specifically related to the Commonwealth and EFTA, is a part, sometimes a very large part,
of a problem that relates to world trade and the world economy as a whole. It is necessary to the European Community,
which depends on healthy world trade for its welfare and on
a peaceful world for its security, that these problems should
be solved. Monnet has always realised that the machinery of
the European Community was only a start and that many of
the most important economic problems can be tackled only
on a larger scale: by moving towards methods of the Community type in the wider world. He has envisaged that the
European Community will play a leading part in this as the
generator of Monnet's revolution. Thus the external policies

that have been considered are not merely a method of pre-cooking negotiations for British entry into the Economic Community, although this is a very important aspect; they are also a part of the creation of a liberal and constructive posture for Europe in the world. This is considered as a whole in Part IV.

There is, then, a practical programme for the British and for the Europeans on the Continent in relation to the Economic Community. The Continentals should keep the Community in being without allowing de Gaulle to turn it into an instrument of his chauvinism. The British should be clearly determined to accept and help to build up the Community method, not only in economics but also in foreign policy and defence; they should also improve their own economic health and vigour. And both Continentals and British should collaborate to ensure that their internal policies do not drift apart and that their external policies are such as to help solve the main problems of Commonwealth and world trade.

If these things, or at least a sufficient proportion of them, are done, then Britain will be credibly available, and the Five consequently better able to win their battles with de Gaulle. A Community-minded Britain will be able to join the Economic Community when they have done so, whether by bending de Gaulle's mind in the face of a possible combination between the Five and Britain; or by the return of a democratic and European government in France; or possibly even by the temporary exit of France from the Community and the entry of Britain instead. In either case, the Economic Community can eventually once more become a foundation for the building of Monnet's Europe and for its extension into Monnet's revolution. But Britain will not be a part of it, nor indeed is the relaunching so likely to happen, unless Britain genuinely accepts the Community method in a broad political sense. For the meantime, as the next two chapters show, the thick of the struggle will lie in politics and defence rather than in economics. The Economic Community is, for the present, not the mainspring of political change, but one feature in a much broader political conflict.

A DEFENCE COMMUNITY

The purpose of a Defence Community: in Monnet's Europe; in Atlantic partnership; in world disarmament

THE mainspring of the endeavour to build Monnet's Europe has been the resolve to finish once and for all with wars between the European peoples. When nations have their own armed forces, war between them is always possible, so a federal system for defence or a Defence Community is an essential part of the European design. Moreover, as the last chapter explained, other essays in the Community method, such as the Economic Community, will never be entirely secure while member-governments dispose of the armed forces with which they can resist the Community's laws. Thus a Defence Community is in the long run basic to the whole federal conception.

As well as being secure from each other's assaults, however, the European peoples must be able to defend themselves against aggression from outside. With Stalin's vast Red Army only a few miles away, the Europeans quickly grasped that their nations separately were helpless. They were shielded by the American commitment to Europe, but the lesson that they would hang separately was not forgotten.

When, therefore, German rearmament was called for in 1950, the Europeans' natural response was to propose a Defence Community within which the German soldiers would be integrated with those from the other European countries. To balance the Germans, however, either the French or the British were needed. The British held aloof. The French Parliament rejected the scheme although the French government had put it forward. So the European Defence Community was still-born.

Europe, having failed to unite for defence, has remained weak and hence dependent on the United States not only in nuclear weapons but also in conventional forces. It is not an easy relationship, for the European nations, feeling that the United States with its great strength holds the responsibility, have failed to provide their fair share of the conventional forces required. Britain and France have been particularly remiss. The Americans, with their balance-of-payments troubles, have naturally become tired of paying out the dollars needed to keep nearly half a million of their troops in Europe for the benefit of its inhabitants, who are bursting with prosperity but too mean and idle to provide their own defence. The European nations, for their part, show more resentment at American dominance than gratitude for the protection. It is a potentially explosive situation.

De Gaulle, with his ingrained hatred of America and envy of anyone more powerful than himself, shows every sign of wanting it to explode. He has removed virtually the whole of the French forces from the NATO system. He rudely rebuffs honest offers by the Americans to consider co-operation in defence. His evident desire to weaken the Atlantic alliance bears out the plan outlined in his *Mémoires de Guerre*, expounding his intention to form a group of Continental nations led by France and probably, at least in the long run, to dispense with the American connection and perhaps replace it by an alliance with Russia.

The reaction of Monnet and the Europeans is the converse. They want to satisfy the desire for Europe to stand on its own feet, and thus to drain the poison of inferiority from its relations with America. But they understand that a coalition of European states on the gaullist pattern will never be united and, hence, strong enough to do this and that a European Defence Community is therefore required. They appreciate, moreover, Europe's fundamental interest in the alliance with America and are therefore determined not to sap it but, on the contrary, to strengthen it by working out a form of partnership that will keep the two sides of the Atlantic permanently together.

The motive behind de Gaulle's conception is the aggrandisement of France, or of a group of nations led by France, by manipulating a balance of power. Monnet's object is the opposite: to bring stability and security to a world that desperately needs them. Thus Monnet believes that the problem of disarmament will be solved only if the Soviet authorities cease to believe in the possibility of achieving a communist

world. "When this becomes so obviously impossible that
nobody, even within a closed society, can any longer believe
it—when the partnership of America and a United Europe
makes it plain to all that the West may change from within
but that others cannot change it by outside pressures, then
Khrushchev or his successor will accept the facts, and the
conditions will at last exist for turning so-called peaceful co-
existence into genuine peace. Then at last real disarmament
will become possible." Monnet goes on to say that we may not
have to wait long for this change. "The history of European
unification shows that when people become convinced a
change is taking place that creates a new situation, they act
on their revised estimate before that situation is established.
. . . Can we not expect a similar phenomenon in the future
relations with the Soviet Union?"[1]

Europe has, indeed, a greater interest in disarmament than
almost any other part of the world, because its dense concentration of people would suffer so terribly in a nuclear war.
But, for the reasons explained by Monnet, if de Gaulle
succeeds in splitting the West he will increase Soviet intransigence and make a real agreement on disarmament less likely.
His disregard for disarmament negotiations and opposition to
the test ban are likewise a serious threat to the security of the
European peoples. A Defence Community, on the other hand,
set up on the lines advocated by Monnet, would help in
several ways to make nuclear war less likely: it would reduce
Europe's reliance on nuclear defence by strengthening its
power to defend itself with conventional weapons; it would
consolidate the Atlantic alliance instead of feeding Russian
intransigence with the hope of its collapse; and the attitude of
Monnet and the majority of the Europeans is anti-chauvinist
and conducive to disarmament and world order.

**Military objectives: strengthen conventional defence; influence
American nuclear policy and guarantee a second strike**

The population of Russia is about 210 million; that of the
European Community, enlarged by the addition of Britain
and the other applicants, some 250 million. Yet even with
nearly half a million American troops in Europe, the European nations are too weak to contemplate meeting a con-

[1] Jean Monnet, "A Ferment of Change", *Journal of Common Market
Studies*, Vol. I, No. 3, p. 210.

ventional attack by Russia without recourse to nuclear arms.

This is partly because the Western democracies, and foremost of them Britain, lack the will to provide, by long enough periods of military conscription and big enough expenditure, the necessary sinews of conventional defence. These democracies should really consider whether a slight restriction of affluence would be too big a price to pay for reducing the risk of nuclear annihilation. But even if they were to match the Russians more closely in numbers and conventional equipment, they lack the unity needed to make them feel secure.

Thus, although the European Defence Community was rejected a decade ago by Britain and France, its logic still remains. Only the establishment of such a Community, with institutions as strong and forces as integrated as were then proposed, will give the European nations the necessary cohesion to enable them to confront the Russians on equal terms and even to lift some of the burden from American shoulders. A recent report of the Western European Union emphasised the advantage of such integration. "Increased expenditure on conventional forces is undoubtedly required as a result of the new strategic doctrine, especially if Europe continues to adhere to the present concept of national forces. If armies, navies and air forces were integrated at the European level, the effectiveness of the European conventional forces would be greatly improved without expenditure rising above present levels."[1] The greater economy and effectiveness of integrated arms production have also been repeatedly stressed.

A European Defence Community still cannot be formed without France or Britain. France in her present mood will not help to set one up. It would therefore be possible only with British participation.

Such participation would be greatly to Britain's advantage. Not only would the defence of Western Europe be strengthened; but the tide would have been turned again in the direction of Monnet's Europe, this time with the British playing a full part. And though the idea of the Defence Community may have been anathema to de Gaulle, he might well swallow his pride and join if he saw France's Continental partners joining and thus cutting themselves off from his *Europe des patries* for good; if he did not, the French, many

[1] Assembly of Western European Union, *Report on a NATO Nuclear Force*, 16 October 1962, p. 13.

of whom are still deeply attached to the European idea, might dispense with him and install once again a European-minded government. In any case, with a Community-minded Britain, the building of Monnet's Europe could continue without France in the 'sixties just as it did without Britain in the 'fifties.

It is quite possible that, were the British to make a genuine offer to set up a Defence Community, the Germans, who would be an essential part of it, would decline. For France is a natural hinterland for Germany's conventional defence, providing lines of communication with America and an area for defence in depth. The Low Countries might provide alternative lines of communication, but manifestly not defence in depth. There would therefore be military objections to such a Community unless France was its ally, and the Germans might fear that de Gaulle would withdraw these facilities if they were to join in establishing such a Community. The Germans, moreover, like other members of the Economic Community, have the habit of thinking in terms of the Six and of assuming that the British have, at best, a long way to go before they can be regarded as fully reliable exponents of the Community method. Thus the British would have to give very convincing proof of their acceptance of the Community method, and also of a changed attitude towards Germany itself, before they could carry with them the Germans along with the other Continentals.

On the other side, the relationship between Germany and America is so close and German awareness of the need for American protection so acute that American support for the idea, which would certainly follow from the contemporary principles of American policy, would carry much weight in a German decision.

Even if the Germans decided against it, the fact that the British were working for Community solutions on this scale would have an electric effect on the political situation in Europe. It might, moreover, be possible to maintain constant pressure on de Gaulle by agreement on the principle of a Defence Community that would come into effect when France as well as the other participants had ratified it.

Adequate conventional defence is extremely important, but public attention is inevitably held by the nuclear weapons of extermination, and these are at the centre of the gaullist controversy. Europe depends on America even more in the nuclear field than in the conventional. The British will have no home-made strategic nuclears when the V-bombers are obsolete. The *force de frappe* is still in its infancy. All the tactical nuclear weapons in Europe are made and controlled by America.

De Gaulle's reaction to this dependence is true to type. He publicly questions the effectiveness of America as an ally: ". . . no one in the world—particularly no one in America— can say if, where, when, how and to what extent the American nuclear weapons would be employed to defend Europe."[1] But this does not lead him to try to make the alliance more effective. Far from it. His tone and behaviour are calculated to weaken the American commitment to Europe. It is, however, doubtful whether his efforts to build strategic nuclear weapons independently of the Atlantic alliance will ever be successful without the help of either Britain or Germany; France alone simply does not have the resources to keep up with the giants. But Britain will not attach her nuclear capacity to a gaullist France that might eventually turn it against America. Nor is Germany likely to allow its industry's drive to be harnessed to the French atomic effort.

Successive British governments have tried to maintain their nuclear independence while co-operating within the Atlantic alliance. When the V-bombers are gone, Britain would, under the Nassau agreement, still have the right to fire her Polaris missiles unilaterally "where Her Majesty's Government may decide that supreme national interests are at stake".[2] But even if the next British government wishes to retain its rights under the Nassau agreement, these Polaris missiles will after some years in turn become obsolete, and Britain's lease of national independence is then most unlikely to be renewed.

In an attempt to satisfy the aspirations of European nations to be masters of their fate the Americans have proposed the fully integrated multilateral force, to which European nations would contribute money and men and over whose disposition they would in return receive a share of control. In line with the American policy of discouraging the spread of independent nuclear armouries, however, the Europeans would under this scheme have no power to press the button.

[1] Press conference held by General de Gaulle, 14 January 1963.
[2] Government White Paper Cmnd 1915, HMSO, December 1962.

Thus de Gaulle wants complete nuclear independence, with overtones of opposition; the British have, during the life of Polaris, the right to press the button when their "supreme interests" are at stake; and the Americans have offered the European nations a multilateral force in which they would just be bus drivers—whose union would, however, have some control over the routes and timetables. There are three other main variants of nuclear policy for Europe: a European Defence Community disposing of its own atomic weapons; a NATO atomic force over whose disposal European nations would have a majority and the United States a minority vote; or the renunciation by Europe of all part in the manufacture, manning or control of nuclear arms. These six variants of policy derive from permutations of the answers to three basic questions. How much effort should European nations put into nuclear defence? How much control should they have over it? And should their policies be formed severally or jointly?

It is possible to conceive the use of strategic nuclears for three main purposes: to retaliate against, and hence to deter, an attack by strategic nuclear weapons; to retaliate against, and hence to deter, an attack by conventional arms with or without tactical nuclear weapons; and to secure other objectives of foreign policy by using or threatening to use them.

It is not hard to assess the first and the third of these. The use of nuclear weapons to threaten other nations instead of to deter aggression is totally inadmissible. No nation should seek the opportunity to do this. Retaliation against a nuclear attack, on the other hand, is the hard core of the theory of deterrence. Every NATO government bases its defence planning upon this doctrine. It is indeed hard to contest; many British unilateralists accept the necessity of the American deterrent for this purpose. Without such a deterrent, one is open to blackmail by a nation possessing nuclear weapons and, to judge from the experience of recent years, the Russian government would not be backward in resorting to such blackmail.

The use of strategic nuclear weapons to deter a conventional attack is more questionable. The British and German governments have argued that, with the West's conventional weakness in relation to Russia, the danger of conventional war is greatly reduced by the fear of nuclear retaliation; and that since a conventional war might escalate, *via* tactical nuclear weapons, to an all-out nuclear war, deterrence against conventional as well as nuclear attack is the safest policy. This argument is reinforced for the Germans by their exposed position which lays them open to devastation even in a conventional war, and *a fortiori* if tactical nuclears are used.

The American administration, on the other hand, with the responsibility for these aweful weapons uppermost in their minds, have evolved the doctrine that the alliance should be able to meet any attack at the level at which it is made : a conventional attack by conventional arms; tactical nuclear weapons by tactical nuclear weapons; and an all-out nuclear attack by strategic nuclear weapons, directed at the enemy's forces or at his cities according to the direction of his own attack. It follows from this doctrine that Europe should, as recommended earlier, increase its conventional strength by integration and by the use of more resources, in order to be a genuine counterweight to Russia. This does not mean that America has renounced her option of nuclear retaliation against a conventional attack, but that her policy is to have the widest possible range of options and above all to avoid being faced with the stark alternatives of capitulation or nuclear annihilation.

Thus the only unquestionable principle of nuclear policy is deterrence against a nuclear attack, and the European nations are consequently entitled to secure for themselves the guarantee of such deterrence, that is to say, a second strike if their territory is struck first by an enemy.

Deterrence against a conventional attack is a more doubtful doctrine, particularly for the European peoples who, as has already been pointed out, are among the most vulnerable in the world to nuclear destruction. It would be so dangerous for them to use strategic nuclear weapons first that their avowed intention to do so would hardly be credible. Despite the understandable fears of the Germans, therefore, and the past policies of the British, the European nations should not wish to have any guarantee of strategic nuclear retaliation against a conventional attack or to dispose of their own means of retaliating in those circumstances. What they can justifiably demand is a greater influence over America's policies in such contingencies, for these policies are clearly a matter of life or death for Europe.

Given the guarantee of a second strike and reasonable influence over nuclear policy as a whole, the European nations should avoid both duplication of effort within the Atlantic alliance and any proliferation of nuclear arsenals.

The European nations will have substantial influence over American policy only if they are united. The history of the Trade Expansion Act shows the truth of this in the economic field; it was only the weight of the Economic Community in world trade that forced this radical change in American policy. A European Defence Community could likewise influence American policy, partly because it would be able to contribute heavily to the defence of the alliance, and partly because the Americans would realise that, if they did not accord it a reasonable degree of influence, there would be the danger of Europe's going it alone—with Europe's great resources a much more credible danger than in the case of gaullist France. But, in order to cut this amount of ice, it would have to be a fully integrated Defence Community, not just a multi-national alliance based on unanimous voting and the right of each member to withdraw his forces when he saw fit.

Much can be done to strengthen the reliability of the American deterrent for Europe without Europe's having its own button to press. The intention to maintain the alliance could be enshrined in a Treaty valid for, say, fifty years. The Americans would be given a material incentive not to withdraw their protection if Europe were to pay a substantial sum each year towards the cost of the deterrent, now estimated at some $15 billion a year. Thus, if Europe were to pay $3-5 billion a year, this would be much less than it would cost Europe to keep in the race on its own but enough to be of considerable interest to Congress and, indeed, enough to eliminate the current weakness of the dollar. Europe could likewise provide men to man the weapons, preferably, as in the proposed multilateral force, in crews of mixed nationality, in which the Americans could play their part like the European nations. These steps could be taken by the separate European states in alliance with America. But, as has been shown in the previous paragraph, Europe's needs are likely to be better satisfied if it acts, in concert with America, as a united European Defence Community.

By such methods the alliance can be made more solid and

durable. It remains conceivable, however, that the two sides of the Atlantic could drift apart, and it would therefore be reassuring for Europe to have a manufacturing option, that is to say, to be able to produce its own weapons within, say, five years should American support be withdrawn, leaving Europe with only the limited life of whatever weapons system was employed by the multilateral force at the time. It is anyway desirable for European industry to have its share of the contracts for making the West's deterrent, for this is a field in which pioneering research and development is done, and American industry will otherwise pull steadily ahead. If Europe were paying its share of the cost of the deterrent, it would be entitled to claim a part of the industrial benefit. This would reduce the advantage to America's balance of payments, though not to her budget, but by then the dollar problem should have been solved by other means.

There remains the question whether Europe should have the physical guarantee of a second strike, in the form of its own button to press if European territory were struck first and America did not immediately respond. Such was the understanding with Britain under the Nassau agreement, although "supreme interests" might be interpreted more widely than this. It seems reasonable that Europe should have a physical guarantee of this sort, provided that independent national deterrents are replaced by a Defence Community. The Americans, for their part, would have an assurance that Europe would not abuse this right if the multilateral force to which the right applied were too small for its use by Europe in a first strike against Russia to be a sane policy, though big enough of course to be a powerful deterrent even should the American deterrent itself fail. The button could at the same time be guarded by both European and American troops, so that Europe could use it illegally, that is to say as a first-strike weapon without American agreement, only by overpowering the Americans and hence committing an act of aggression against them, which would probably be followed at the least by the withdrawal of American support from Europe, thus placing on Europe the full burden of its own nuclear programme in order to have nuclear protection at all. In short, this limited right and power to press its own button for a second strike could be arranged in such a way that the possibility of its abuse was minimal.

The problem of tactical nuclear weapons is not dissimilar, although their scale is so much less horrific. Europe can hardly forgo this element of its armoury, because the Russians have them and if they used them, European troops could not be expected to stand and fight with conventional arms alone. It would be most desirable for Europe to have a no-first-strike policy in this field as well, for the European peoples could suffer very severely from the use of tactical nuclear even though this did not escalate to strategic weapons. Yet such is Europe's conventional weakness at present that adequate defence against a conventional attack would not be possible without the tactical nuclears. This underlines again the urgency for Europe of organising a conventional defence that is strong and united enough to meet a Russian attack without the virtual suicide of making it into a nuclear war.

Europe is not the only theatre in which the use of tactical nuclear arms may be contemplated. It might, for example, be impossible to contain a Chinese attack on India or, eventually, on Australia without them. American support would almost certainly be forthcoming in either of these cases, but if for any reason it was not, Europe's possession of tactical nuclear arms could provide the only means of checking such an aggression.

In both conventional and nuclear defence, then, Europe's needs can be met only in the context of a Defence Community. Europe's participation in the nuclear deterrent, moreover, should be as closely as possible interwoven with America's in an intimate and enduring partnership. In these ways Europe, whose peoples are sick of war and have a deep interest in the maintenance of peace, can provide for its defence in a way that minimises the danger of a conflict's breaking out.

A Political Community; the British contribution; the defeat of de Gaulle

If national armed forces are to be integrated into a European force, they need to be put under a supranational or federal political control. They cannot be left without political masters. A coalition working by unanimity is impossibly unwieldy, agreeing, as Kennan says, "only on what not to do". A Community control is therefore the only practical possibility.

When the European Defence Community was planned in the early 'fifties, this problem was confronted and it was proposed to establish a European Political Community, with a Parliament and Council of Ministers, to whom the Defence Commission and, incidentally, the High Authority of the Coal and Steel Community would have been responsible. It is hard to envisage any very different method of control whenever a Defence Community may in the future be set up.

The disposal of conventional forces by such a body presents no exceptional difficulties, although it may be doubted whether a qualified majority is not too clumsy a mechanism to produce the swift and clear decisions that are required in time of war, and whether voting by simple majority should not therefore be introduced, perhaps after a transitional period. The taking of decisions relating to the use of nuclear weapons, and especially strategic nuclears, is however a more difficult question. There is so little warning of a nuclear attack that a decision may be needed in a very few minutes.

Under the system proposed above, Europe would have no right to decide to fire unless its territory had first been struck. If a nuclear attack were verified, there would be no question but that Europe should retaliate. The decision could therefore be made by permanent representatives of the Ministers, at the headquarters of the Defence Community, on receiving evidence of the attack and in the light of standing orders about retaliation in such circumstances. In all other cases there would be time for a meeting of Ministers and, indeed, they would not have the power to decide whether or not to fire but only in what direction to exert their influence on America. Thus there seem to be no insuperable problems arising out of the Community method of control.

It would not be possible to create an integrated conventional force or a multilateral nuclear force overnight. Indeed, five years might be a reasonable period for the transition. During this time the forces would still be largely multinational, and it would not be essential for the Community to take its decisions by majority vote. This could, therefore, be a period comparable to stages one and two of the Economic Community, during which most decisions are still taken by unanimity, and the members become used to working together on these problems. The Community would necessarily move over to majority decisions at the end of that transitional period, when the forces had become fully integrated.

But all such plans for Political and Defence Community are impractical unless France or Britain or both subscribe to them. If de Gaulle is unlikely to volunteer for this in the conventional field, it is out of the question that he would do so in the nuclear. "France intends to have its national defence ...for a great people to have the free disposition of itself and the means to struggle to preserve it is an absolute imperative." "Thus principles and realities combine to lead France to equip itself with an atomic force of its own." "...the principle...which consists in disposing in our own right of our deterrent force...To turn over our weapons to a multilateral force, under a foreign command, would be to act contrary to that principle of our defence and our policy."[1] For the time being, the Defence Community will be set up only if the British agree.

It is in their interest to do so. This has already been argued in respect to conventional forces. The case in the nuclear field is stronger. Britain's independent deterrent is a wasting asset. Does anybody believe that, when Polaris is obsolete, the arrangement would be repeated with another weapons system? One simple statistic shows that Britain on its own is such a lightweight that it might just as well be out of the ring : the American nuclear budget is equal to about three times the total British defence budget of which only a tenth is said to be spent on nuclear arms—a disproportion of thirty to one.

But Britain's nuclear capacity is substantial enough to be the basis on which Europe could negotiate with America an arrangement of the type outlined above : for greater European influence over the disposal of a multilateral force and for the guarantee of a second strike with it. Britain itself was able to negotiate as much and more at Nassau, probably the last time she would be able to do so. Britain with a number of Continental countries would be able to secure these rights for a long period, and to justify them indefinitely by the weight of the European contribution to the alliance.

To do this would require a radical change in British policies and attitudes. The predominant British reaction to the proposal for a multilateral force was one of horror at the idea of ships manned by men of two nationalities. The thought of

[1] Extracts from General de Gaulle's press conference, 14 January 1963.

foreigners in British ships may be offensive to naval tradition
—although it has been pointed out that Nelson's *Victory* had
a very cosmopolitan crew. But it is essential in a multilateral
force to ensure, by physical means, that it really is multilateral : that national contingents are not permanently withdrawn, or pulled out at the critical moment and made to fire
their missiles independently. In a multinational force this
possibility cannot be excluded; indeed, if gaullist France were
to participate in such a force, which the NATO allies seem
so eager to see happen, de Gaulle's record during the last war
and since shows that unilateral action would be only too
likely to occur. The British government too has insisted on the
right of independent action, presumably because it might wish
to exercise it. Yet the possibility of independent action by each
main contributor to a multinational force sharply reduces its
credibility and weight, and at the same time increases the
danger of a button's being pressed at the wrong time. If it is
accepted that for these reasons the whole of Europe's contribution to the nuclear effort of the alliance, for which it is to
get its influence over policy and guarantee of a second strike,
should be made collectively, then the multilateral force, mixed
crews and all, is necessary and the British will have to cease
being horrified by the thought of foreigners in British ships
and turn their minds to constructive thinking on how to
select and train efficient crews.

If they cannot summon the courage to take the plunge, the
British can accustom themselves to the water in easy stages :
first, a minimal contribution to the multilateral force as proposed by the Americans; *second*, a big contribution made at
the same time as the independent deterrent is scrapped; *third*,
the incorporation in a European Defence Community of the
European nations' contribution to the force. It would be best
to go the whole way at once, but the easy stages are also a
viable route.

This is the last high card that Britain has to play, but it is
the ace of trumps. In the field of economics, de Gaulle,
ensconced in the Economic Community, is playing from
strength; he has the veto on his side. In defence, the
institutions of the alliance do not work in his favour
for he has no veto over the actions of the others; his
force de frappe is less credible than the British deterrent; and
the Germans have shown, by their agreement on the multi-

lateral force, that they regard the Americans and not de
Gaulle as their essential ally. German commitment to this
force stands in the way of de Gaulle's harnessing German
industry to his *force de frappe*; a European Defence Community including Germany, Britain and other nations wishing and eligible to take part would exclude this possibility for
good.

Defence, not economics, is what interests de Gaulle. A
European Defence Community that excluded France would
put paid to his hopes of a European coalition led by France
that would "contract alliances with one side or the other"
and act as the "arbiter between the Soviet and Anglo-Saxon
camps".[1] It is possible that, in these circumstances, he himself
would climb down, believing that it was better for France to
play its part in the new Community than to remain in isolation. If he did not, there can be little doubt that the French
people would sooner or later abandon gaullism and return to
the Community fold.

If the British fail to make their choice in favour of a
Defence Community, then it is to be hoped that the French
will still, having got gaullism out of their system, come round
themselves in time to doing so. But with Britain or France, or
preferably and in the long run almost certainly with both,
such a Community would represent a decisive and irreversible
step on the road towards Monnet's Europe and away from
chauvinistic nationalism.

[1] General de Gaulle, *Mémoires de Guerre 1944–46*, Plön, p. 179, 1959.

10

A POLITICAL COMMUNITY

A Community system for economics, foreign policy and defence: based on a convention of human rights; the need to persuade Britain or France

THE essence of Monnet's Europe is the transfer of political power in certain matters from national governments to new European institutions. It has been explained how this principle has been qualified and softened in the Communities: how the national governments still take the main decisions, but acting collectively by majority vote in the new institutions instead of separately; and how power has been transferred only in respect to matters where there are compelling reasons for the change. But the transfer of power from national to European institutions is real and should not be underplayed: on the contrary, the replacement of national autarchy by common decisions and common action is the object of the whole endeavour.

Any such transfer of power is a political act. The Economic Community is a political Community because it transfers power in matters of such political consequence as tariffs, agricultural policies, cartels and monopolies. But the term Political Community has frequently been used in a more special sense. A European Political Community has been proposed in recent years that would deal with questions of foreign policy as a whole, apart from those important economic sectors of foreign policy that are the preserve of the Economic Community. And in 1953, a Draft Treaty for a European Political Community was prepared which would have been responsible for defining the foreign policy of the Six in those fields relating to the scope of the proposed Defence Community and of the Coal and Steel Community. Thus the term EPC has been used to denote a Community concerned with some sectors of the foreign policy of its members.

The name Political Community has, however, also been

used in a more general sense, to describe the roof or umbrella for a number of specialised Communities. At present there are three Communities: the Economic Community, the Coal and Steel Community and Euratom. Communities for defence and for foreign policy have also been proposed. If these were all set up separately, and there is much to be said for this rather than for adding to the functions of the Economic Community, then it would be essential for their activities to be co-ordinated. This could most effectively be done by a Political Community whose independent executive would comprise the Presidents of the executives—Commission or High Authority—of each specialised Community and whose Council of Ministers would consist of the Prime Ministers of each member-government. The European Parliament and Court of Justice would be related to the executive and Council of the Political Community, as they are to those of each specialised Community. Thus, a somewhat familiar system of government would be projected on to the European plane, with specialised Communities corresponding to Ministries in national governments, and with the institutions of the Political Community as a kind of federal government.

Whether the federal system is set up in this way, however, or whether it is done by adding functions to the Economic Community, the term Political Community is used in this book to denote a Community responsible for the main matters of common concern to the members, chiefly in defence, foreign policy and economics: in fact, the political expression of Monnet's Europe.

The reconstruction of Europe's political system in this way is a vast undertaking. The reasons why, despite the magnitude of the task, it is being attempted were explained in chapter 2. Most people would still say it was impossible, had Monnet and the Europeans not already the astounding achievement of the Economic Community to their credit. Now it seems, if the battle with gaullism is won, that this idealist's dream is as likely as not to be realised.

If such a recasting of the structure of power is contemplated and not unlikely to be undertaken, it is necessary to consider the principles according to which this power should be used: the view of man as a political and social being on which the Community's laws are to be based. For as soon as a Community disposes of a preponderance of physical power

—a certain stage in the development of an integrated Defence Community is the watershed—its treatment of its citizens becomes of paramount importance to them. The principles by which such treatment is to be guided are usually enshrined in constitutions in a declaration of rights. In Europe, the Strasbourg Declaration of Human Rights lies ready to hand. It should be part of the constitution of a European Political Community, with fully effective means for its enforcement in all countries that become full members.

In the shrinking world of today, the different peoples interact so intensively on and with each other that the relations between them are as important as the relations between the citizens of any one state. The European Community is a living proof of this. But it is true of the relations not only between European peoples but also between the peoples of Europe and those of other continents. There is a supranational Community in Europe because the fact of their interdependence has sunk deep into the political understanding of the European peoples. In the world as a whole, however, science with its fruits of transport, communications and weapons of extermination has raced ahead of political understanding and there is no Community to regulate the consequent interaction between the nations.

For these reasons, it would be appropriate for a Community that is built on an understanding of the interdependence between peoples in the modern world to base its work not only on a declaration of the rights of its own citizens but also on a statement of its attitude towards the citizens of states outside. It is notable that, in the preamble to the Treaty establishing the European Economic Community, three out of the eight clauses refer to the Community's attitude towards third countries: "Desirous of contributing by means of a common commercial policy to the progressive abolition of restrictions on international trade"; "Intending to confirm the solidarity which binds Europe and overseas countries and desiring to ensure the development of their prosperity in accordance with the principles of the Charter of the United Nations"; and "... calling upon the other peoples of Europe who share in their ideals to join in their efforts"—an aspiration that has temporarily come to grief on the Treaty's anti-federal provision for the veto on new members. A Treaty establishing a Political Community could valuably contain a coherent

declaration of the principles on which it would base its behaviour towards other peoples, which should be those of
Monnet's revolution, as well as a more orthodox declaration of
the rights of its own citizens.

It has been shown how the EEC, to quote again from its
preamble, was established as the "foundations of an ever closer
union among the European peoples", and how de Gaulle has
now thrown a barrier across this royal road towards a Political
Community. The behaviour of the Europeans and the Five
within the institutions of the Economic Community can still
decide the fate of Monnet's Europe. If their resistance to de
Gaulle were to cave in, the battle against gaullism would have
been lost; while if, after 1965, they use their power to cut
tariffs against the will of de Gaulle or his successor, they will
have done much to rescue Monnet's revolution. It has also
been explained how Britain's availability, by providing an
alternative to France, helps the Five to do these things. But de
Gaulle's barrier cannot be thrown aside within the context of
the Economic Community alone, unless de Gaulle pulls France
out of it, which he is unlikely to do, and a Community-minded
Britain joins in her place; or unless France is converted again
to the paths of Monnet's Europe. Unless and until either of
these things happens, the Economic Community is a part of
the background against which a battle will be fought out in
the fields of defence and of the political structure of Europe;
and British availability for the Economic Community is a factor
that enables the Europeans and the Five to fight more bravely
in these fields as well as in that of economics: the power of
this factor depending on how federalist the British have
become.

The concept of a Defence Community has been considered
and it has been shown that, so long as gaullist France blocks
the further development of the Community idea, a decision by
Britain to put her defence effort into such a Community along
with those other European nations wishing to take part would
be the only quick way to relaunch Monnet's Europe, almost
certainly bringing France as well back to the fold in a short
time. But nobody could or should conceal from the British
people that this would in fact be an irrevocable decision to
take part in Monnet's Europe with its full implications of
eventual federation. This is a decision that can be taken only
on the basis of a conviction that it is advantageous and right

to take part in a Political Community. The question has to be seen as a whole and thrashed out in public discussion. During the negotiations for British entry to the Economic Community, partly because there was not enough time to accustom people to such a radical idea and partly because of Macmillan's own preference for playing it cool, the economic issues were not seen by the public in their full political context, which was dismissed by the British government in a few vague generalities. Much of the sourness in public debate on the subject could be attributed to a failure to understand the full reasons for the big change that was being proposed and a feeling that there were nevertheless some such reasons that were not being fully explained. The same mistake must not be made again and, indeed, if participation in a Defence Community is to be considered, the political implications can hardly be evaded. The British government would have first to decide in principle, with the full knowledge of the British people, in favour of participating in a European Political Community.

Thus, neither of the two main legs of a Political Community — Defence Community and the Economic Community—can provide the basis for advance towards Monnet's Europe until either Britain or France, or both, has decided to accept a Political Community as its objective. When either of these nations does so, a relaunching of Monnet's Europe can be organised. Meanwhile, the task is to keep the Europeans and the Five resisting gaullism, while the British and French are persuaded that the idea of the Political Community is right.

Until Britain or France is persuaded: public discussion, diplomatic activity, cultural exchange

For such a radical reform of political structure as the creation of a Political Community, it is not enough just to press governments for a decision. The individuals and groups that actively form and propagate opinions must be persuaded that it is necessary and, in a democracy, the majority of the nation must find the idea not unpalatable.

Any far-reaching step towards a Political Community, such as the establishment of a Defence Community, will therefore have to be preceded by an exhaustive public discussion of the issue. On the Continent, the federal idea has been before the public for some fifteen years; in Britain there have been about two years' debate on the Economic Community. During this

time an immense flood of words flowed on the subject, which
was given very full public consideration. But the British need
to reflect more upon the whole idea of Monnet's Europe
before they can wholeheartedly embrace it with all its
implications.

In France, the "classe politique" was overwhelmingly favourable to the concept of a federal Europe but de Gaulle is
against it and has, for the time being, reduced the political
parties to impotence. It is not clear how many of the people
who now vote for him would continue to do so if they saw
that he was likely to wreck the European construction in
which France has properly taken such pride. It is certainly not
likely that they would vote for gaullist successors if they knew
that this was the probable result of their policies. The Europeans in France, who are able and numerous, must therefore
explain this to the French people so that, after de Gaulle, they
can revert to their role among the leaders of Monnet's Europe.
The Five and the British can help considerably by acting in
such a way that gaullist policies do not succeed.

The governments of the Five are still on the whole supporters of Monnet's Europe, although Adenauer has gone
along with de Gaulle and Erhard is more interested in free
trade than in Community institutions. But if a viable scheme
for a Defence and Political Community were proposed to
them by post-gaullist France or, after a further process of conversion to the concept of Monnet's Europe, by Britain, they
would be likely to accept. It is nevertheless necessary to keep
the ideas of Monnet's Europe clear and sharp in the public
mind in these countries, so that they will not lose sight of the
alternative consequences of these ideas and of de Gaulle's
challenge to them, and so that they can play their full part in
persuading the British and French.

For, although each nation has to conduct its own debate in
terms of its own traditions, interests and ideas, the debate must
also take place on the European plane. A major factor in the
decision to establish a Political Community is the attitude of
the different potential members towards its construction and to
the main issues with which it would be likely to have to deal,
and these things must therefore be discussed between them;
and the traffic of ideas across frontiers, which has always been
an essential part of European history, is now much heavier
and more necessary than ever before. Those who have thought

deeply about the problems of Monnet's Europe and who have experienced its ideas in action, and they are naturally mostly citizens of the Community Six, have the right and the duty to explain these things to those who do not yet understand them, whether in the Community itself or in other European countries and, particularly, in Britain where a conversion to the Community method could be the catalyst for a relaunching of Monnet's Europe.

While the process of persuasion and decision is taking place, there is much that governments can do to create a favourable climate for it. For those governments, such as the British, that are not ready to think in terms of a Political Community, such measures must be useful either as acts of co-operation in themselves or as the policies of an applicant to join the Economic Community whose application is in suspense, as well as helping to create the conditions for the future establishment of a Political Community. This does not, however, much limit the field, for there is vast scope for useful collaboration in Europe whatever its ultimate purpose.

For the Six, the continued establishment of the Common Market and the maintenance of the Communities' institutions intact are the first necessity. If de Gaulle, by legal or illegal means, makes the Communities impossible to work, there is nothing to be done except start again with Britain or with post-gaullist France; but it would probably be a death blow to hopes of an eventual Political Community if one of the Five were to destroy the existing Communities.

Chapter 8, which analysed the economic issues, went on to describe the things that could be done to keep Britain available as a potential member of the Economic Community. These are the same things as would create a favourable climate of opinion on both sides of the Channel on the idea of a Political Community. If the Continentals see the British making their economy viable and lopping away the anomalies in their agriculture and taxation policies; if the British see the Continentals ready to take their interests as a potential member into account when framing new Community policies; and if both collaborate on matters of external trade and monetary policy, as is suggested in chapters 11 and 12, then official policies will be moving in the right direction and the impression on public opinion will be good.

In defence, the British would make a strong impact on

Continental, and especially German, opinion if they were to
bring the British Army of the Rhine up to strength; BAOR
has for years been consistently below the level of the British
undertaking to the Western European Union. It would be
better still if they were to increase this commitment, probably
by reintroducing conscription. This would, as explained in
chapter 9, help to reduce the risk of nuclear war and would
make Britain's commitment to Europe clear in a very tangible
way. Exchanges of troops and at staff level between the different European armed forces are also of symbolic as well as
practical value. Objections to the bringing of German troops
to other countries such as Britain are crassly stupid, for if
there is a danger that Germany would again become militarist,
which after the recent experience of the Germans seems im-
probable, it would be greatly increased by keeping the German
Army secluded within German frontiers.

Outside the fields of economics and defence, there is a number of things that a British government could do to foster good
relations with the Continent. A decision to support the building of a Channel tunnel or bridge if the French government
does the same; conversion to the metric system and to a
decimal coinage; a reform of the methods of dealing with
foreigners entering Britain so as to conform more closely to the
good manners with which one is received by immigration and
customs officials on the Continent : such things as these would
be good in themselves and would maintain a sense of momentum in the evolution of relations between Britain and the
Continent.

In addition to official initiatives such as these, and probably
more important, there is much that can be done to encourage
people from the different European countries to meet with
each other and discover their common interests. Ever since the
war the French government has had a powerful programme
for exchanges of this sort with the Germans. Year after year
there have been large numbers of German students in French
universities, French professors lecturing in Germany, meetings
of French and German teachers, journalists, young people and
other groups, and these activities have been promoted by
heavy official subsidies. The Franco-German Treaty provides
for further encouragement to such meetings and to other
activities with a similar purpose. This massive and sustained
campaign has contributed to the Franco-German reconcilia-

tion which is now a sheet-anchor of German policy and attitude towards the postwar world. De Gaulle has tried to abuse
this stock of goodwill by getting the Germans, through the
mechanism of the Franco-German Treaty, to align their
policies with his own instead of hammering them out with
Germany's partners in the Economic Community and in
NATO, although the Germans have shown by their Preamble
to the Treaty that they intend to resist him; but previous
French governments had invested in this programme of cultural exchanges with the genuine intention of laying the
foundations for a better Europe by ending the enmity of the
two chief antagonists.

The French have not of course been alone in undertaking
such activities. Other governments have done so, as have unofficial bodies such as the European Movement and many
municipalities, professional associations and other voluntary
groups. But the French effort has been new in its scope and
its deliberate development as an arm of foreign policy. In the
present situation, where it is necessary to stop the European
peoples from drifting apart and, on the contrary, to bring
home to them a sense of their common interests, it is up to
all governments and private bodies that do not want to see a
Europe of squabbling and jealous *patries*, to make a similar
effort on the European plane.

The programme of cultural exchanges—despite its overtones of Morris dancing and madrigals, there seems to be no
better term to describe this promotion of encounters between
peoples on a wide front—should indeed be recognised as an
essential part of the process of creating a Community or
federation of nations. It is useless just to devise a treaty or
constitution and expect it to work. It will be accepted and
properly applied only if the participants understand each
other's minds and find enough agreement on basic issues : if
they are conscious of each other's sensitive points and vital
interests, so that unnecessary insults and conflicts can be
avoided. Unless it is deliberately fostered, this degree of understanding is not likely to be reached between a group of nations
whose acute national consciousness is a highly centrifugal
force. Thus cultural exchanges on a large scale are necessary
if the climate is to be created in which Communities can be
established and can work.

These arguments are valid within the Six. They apply more

strongly as between Britain and the Continent, in view of Britain's isolation from a decade of the Community experiment and the danger that the British, having been kicked in the teeth as a reward for their well-intentioned efforts to bridge the gap, will turn sour about Monnet's Europe and be lost to it for ever. The British government should put big resources into a programme of exchanges. It should arrange, or aid voluntary bodies that arrange, meetings and conferences between British and Continental groups with common interests, including business people, professional bodies, young people and Members of Parliament; encourage the teaching of Continental languages in Britain and English on the Continent; expand the information services of the British Council and the BBC. It could offer a home for the European University, the project for which is still unhappily hanging in the air. The emphasis should be on the search for common interests and mutual understanding, not just on increasing the prestige of Britain abroad.

Still more valuable than the independent initiatives of governments and private bodies would be multilateral, or failing that bilateral, agreement between governments on the launching of programmes of exchanges. A multilateral treaty, confined to the subject of cultural exchanges, could be concluded between a minimum of three countries and remain open to accession by any that did not join at first. It would have symbolic value, as an earnest of intentions to persevere with the open concept of Monnet's Europe. If it provided for the allocation of substantial resources, it would have the practical value indicated above. And it would neither cut across the activities of the existing Communities or of NATO, nor demand acceptance of the full federal implications of a Political Community before the French or the British were ready to accept them.

Following on the bombshell of the Franco-German Treaty, there has been a spate of proposals for treaties to counteract it. These should be resisted unless they are either multilateral and without provision for vetoes, or unpolitical, or specifically designed to further the Community method. For in a Europe in which the Community method has been evolving as the predominant form of international organisation, the injection of the bilateral treaty is a retrograde step. It is no accident that these treaties are much loved by dictators : they are the symbol of a power relationship between one nation state and another, preferably between the dictator's nation and a weaker one; for, as Bismarck said, one of the parties to such a treaty is usually the rider and one the horse. If de Gaulle's Treaty were answered by others in a similar vein, the European peoples would have been provoked into becoming the Europe of discordant *patries* that they have made such magnificent efforts to leave behind.

Those governments that do accept in principle the concept of a Political Community could, however, strengthen their position by concluding among themselves a Treaty that stated this to be the object of their European policies and provided for negotiations to establish a Political Community to be opened when enough countries had adhered to the Treaty. The Treaty could at the same time make it plain that de Gaulle's attempts to sweep aside the Community method and replace it by coalition or hegemony would fail, if it were to state that signatories would not agree to any so-called political union that did not provide definitely for the introduction of the Community method. Like many dictators before him, de Gaulle works by exploiting the fears and weaknesses of those around him; the countries of the Continent will help to remove those fears and weaknesses if they proclaim unequivocally that they will not be bullied into accepting a type of organisation for Europe that they think to be wrong.

The proclamation of intentions and the imprinting of political ideas on the public mind is, indeed, the essential groundwork for a great political venture. Those governments that want a Political Community cannot further their cause unless they make their beliefs clear, and preferably dramatically clear, whenever an opportunity offers itself; and those such as the British who, while still unconvinced that more than intergovernmental co-operation is required, have the vision of a liberal Europe that would be a force for good in the world at large, should do the same. Bodies such as the Assemblies of the Council of Europe and the Western European Union as well as the Community's European Parliament provide suitable forums, and Europe's major political figures should use them more. Statements and speeches—even press conferences —on other occasions should be made with the express intention of making an impression on the people of Europe as a whole.

When Britain or France has decided: advance through Economic or Defence Community; a political campaign for a Political Community

If, as a result of all the work described above, neither Britain nor France decides in favour of a Political Community, then Europe's future and that of the Western world will probably take one of the forms depicted in chapter 4 : an American hegemony over a discontented and ineffective Europe, with rather dim prospects for the West in the long term; or a rupture of the Atlantic alliance, with the possibility of a rapid advance of communism and decline of the West. But it is to be hoped, and indeed assumed unless it is proved wrong, that Britain or France and preferably both will sooner or later be persuaded that Monnet's Europe represents the only reasonable course.

When that happens there will be a road forward to a Political Community through its two main pillars of the Economic and a Defence Community. But in order that the impetus can be generated for this to take place after de Gaulle's hiatus of bewilderment and bitterness, and in order that progress will not again be blocked by chauvinist reaction, the relaunching of Monnet's Europe should take place with a flourish of trumpets rather than a brandishing of technocrats' brief-cases and slide-rules. The governments that want to take part, and particularly the British and French, should apply the electoral rather than the diplomatic parts of their minds to the problem. They will be embarking on a process of change that will reach into every corner of national life and will be impossible without the assent of a big majority of those who determine the course of political action : political parties, opinion-formers, electorates, each in their different way. They will, especially if de Gaulle or a gaullist successor rules France, encounter an active and able opposition. The enterprise is not likely to succeed unless the kind of thinking and energy are put into it, at both European and national levels, that political parties put into the fighting of elections. Diplomacy derived from a tradition of transacting business with monarchs and oligarchies is not enough—not nearly enough. Debate and persuasion must take place through the political process as a whole, both within the European nations and at those many official and unofficial points at which they now interact.

For, in order that such a transformation of Europe can take

place, it will be necessary to project a vision of the kind of Europe that we want to see: internally, based on solidarity, democracy and human rights; externally, harnessing Europe's energies to the creation of a humane and liberal world order. Such a Europe, not the atavistic power-hungry Europe of gaullist *patries*, is basically suited to the needs of modern European society: war-weary, prosperous and increasingly democratic and liberal. But de Gaulle or others like him can reawaken the emotions and instincts of the past unless the nature of Monnet's Europe is understood and accepted by every open mind. This Part of the book has tried to show its internal nature; the next Part considers the posture of this Europe in the world.

PART IV

TOWARDS WORLD ORDER

11

ATLANTIC PARTNERSHIP

Monnet's revolution and world order; Atlantic partnership the first step; in defence, economics, politics

THE internal structure of Monnet's Europe has now been described. It has been shown that many of the ills which have beset Europe in this century will be cured if de Gaulle's challenge is repulsed and the advance of the Community method is resumed. But Monnet's Europe will not in itself protect the peoples of Europe, any more than those of other continents, against the fearful dangers that the progress of science has discharged upon this age : above all the population explosion and the hydrogen bomb.

Chapter 3 explained how Monnet's revolution, not so much an automatic consequence of a European Community as an act of will on the part of liberal Europeans, could help to establish the world order within which these problems of poverty and insecurity could be solved. For there are no real solutions without common institutions within which the nations can collaborate effectively; and it is the Europeans' special contribution to point the way to their establishment.

De Gaulle, as hostile to any such constructive ideas on the world plane as in Europe, has with his veto on Britain sabotaged the beginnings of Monnet's revolution, and it is certain that he will contest its progress at every step. For the striving towards a world order in which the excessive powers of nation-states are checked so that the common problems of the peoples can be solved by common action is even more anathema to him than the building of Community Europe, in which France is at least top nation for the time being.

The Europeans and the West must fight back against gaullism as much on the wider issues as they do for the European Community; for each is an integral part of the vision of a world in which the critical problems thrust upon us by science are effectively dealt with by methods of collaboration instead of domination. The case for Monnet's Europe will not be understood and may go by default if this vision is not made crystal clear.

In addition to this essential task of projecting as sharply as possible the antithesis between gaullism and the Community method, there is much practical work that can be done to make progress towards a satisfactory world order, even before gaullism is given the *coup de grâce* in Europe. Although the evolution of Monnet's Europe has already indicated what a stimulus it could be, through the spillover effect of Monnet's revolution, to the development of such a world order, the processes of creating a world Community and of establishing one in Europe are at least to some extent independent. The need to solve world problems is so urgent that all possible steps in that direction should be taken, even while Europe is in a state of disarray.

Practical co-operation on international questions will, moreover, contribute towards victory over de Gaulle in Europe. It has been shown that co-operation between European governments can help to improve the climate for a return to the Community method and that if a number of external economic problems were wholly or partly solved, Britain's availability for the Economic Community would become more credible and the balance of advantage in the Community be correspondingly tilted against de Gaulle. More important, perhaps, than either of these two factors, the substance of Monnet's revolution would begin to be hammered on the anvil of experience into the shape of European habits and policies, so that one could predict with some certainty that, de Gaulle once out of the way, the Europeans would throw their energies into the task of building a better world rather than content themselves with the admirable but more limited achievement of curing Europe's internal disorders.

Monnet has long made plain his belief that equal collaboration with America would be the first consequence of a united Europe; and he has stated that this would be "not an end in itself" but "the beginning of the road towards the more orderly world we must have if we are to escape destruction".[1] The basis of collaboration to this end is sound. Europe and America have a common interest in Monnet's revolution and the creation of a humane and democratic world order; together

[1] Second World Congress of Man-made Fibres, London, 1 May 1962.

they have much of the power to create it; if they are at odds, it cannot be done.

In strategic terms, the two have a common interest, first in a system of defence that will counterbalance the power of Russia, and then in the establishment of world security through multilateral and controlled disarmament. Together their strength ensures the first which, as Monnet has explained, is a precondition for the second. If, on the contrary, they are separated, Western Europe will be weak; Russia will be correspondingly strong; its ideological line will be harder; nuclear weapons will proliferate; and, for the latter two reasons, it is scarcely possible to believe that disarmament will come about.

In economics, it is the interest of both Europe and America that the economy of the West should be stable and vigorous and, for political reasons more than economic, that the emergent nations should be prosperous. As the world's two predominant units of demand and suppliers of capital, they can, if they organise their strength effectively, create the conditions under which these objectives can be fulfilled. If they oppose each other, or even if they fail to work constructively together, the centrifugal forces of economic autarchy will prevail; the danger of world slump will always be present and the problems of the emergent nations will remain neglected.

Politically, the two sides of the Atlantic have equal need of the more orderly world that Monnet envisages, not only in order to escape destruction but also to supersede the barbarous anarchy of the world of nation-state leviathans that is repugnant to a liberal and democratic civilisation. Together, they can weld their economic and strategic policies into a powerful force in favour of world order. If they are against each other, the field is open to chaos and the destruction of civilisation either by the hydrogen bomb or through the imposition of a totalitarian authority.

Thus it would be a disaster if de Gaulle were to succeed in sabotaging the Atlantic alliance, and consistent collaboration between Europe and America is an essential basis for world order.

It has been explained in chapter 6 why an Atlantic hegemony, with the United States dominating a number of separate European states, is an unsatisfactory form for such collaboration, and how this is agreed not only by the Europeans but also by the American administration.

Nor is a supranational Community on the pattern of the European Communities suitable, at least for the present, despite the similar background of Europe and America, each stemming from the same roots and each sharing, in varying degree, the decentralised economies and democratic government that go to make up a plural society. The same reasons that work against a hegemony of separate nations militate more strongly against a hegemony within supranational institutions, which would resemble an empire more closely than a democracy. If, on the other hand, domination is mitigated or avoided because Europe is united, it is hard to see how a Community or federal system consisting of two very powerful members and a few much smaller ones could work. Either America, with its greater economic strength and political cohesion, would dominate the European side despite its new unity; or there would be the danger of a deadlock with each side vetoing any clear and constructive policy. Even if the system were to work, it would be liable to make a world order more difficult to achieve because it would itself be such a predominantly powerful unit. If the West had its back to the wall in a struggle against a predominantly hostile world, then such a risk would have to be taken. But so long as there is a reasonable hope of advance towards a democratic world order, based not on the domination of the world by one of its parts but on a reasonable balance between them, it would be foolish of the West to rule out this prospect by forming so vast and powerful a unit that all other nations would shy away from associating with it in a world Community.

There is, in any event, no need to cross this bridge at present. Because America feels strong and Europe is weak, neither is prepared to merge sovereignty with the other. A looser and less irrevocable form of collaboration than a Community is therefore required. Further developments need not be decided until there has been time to test the working of this collaboration and to judge the trend of the West's position in the world.

For these reasons the concept of partnership is being evolved. Its purpose is to organise collaboration as powerfully and constantly as is possible without the permanent transfer of power that is the essence of a Community. It is clear that this should be done by means of a number of long-term contracts between the partners on important matters of mutual concern.

It is not so commonly realised that this partnership will not work unless there is a conscious effort to harmonise the attitudes and opinions of the partners on the most important problems that confront them : the attitudes and opinions not just of governments, but also of those sectors of the public that influence the governments' policies, which in democracies include for the broadest issues the whole electorate. The nature of such an effort has been considered in chapter 10 under the term "cultural exchanges", the purpose of such exchanges being to enable groups of citizens from each partner to discover, by personal contact, their common interests and to determine what common action can be undertaken to satisfy them.

As within Europe, such cultural exchanges already take place across the Atlantic. In the long run, the most effective schemes are probably the Fulbright fellowships and Rhodes scholarships, under which some of the most promising students of each generation cross the Atlantic to study in universities on the other side. But in order to support a partnership, a much more massive and comprehensive effort is required, with intensive contacts between representatives of all sectors of society. Since the cost of transatlantic travel is a serious deterrent to the general public, there is a strong case for its subsidisation in order to extend mutual knowledge as widely as possible.

Equal partnership will not be possible while de Gaulle obstructs Monnet's Europe. But analysis of the different fields for collaboration shows that many things can be done meanwhile to keep Europe and America from drifting apart and to begin to implement the programme of common policies which will be fully possible only when the Community method in Europe has got the better of de Gaulle.

The ideal form of partnership in defence has been sketched out in chapter 9. The defence efforts of Europe and America would be integrated as far as is consistent with the autonomy of the partners. In conventional arms, a European Defence Community would contribute a weight equivalent to that of the United States; in strategic nuclear weapons, this Community would earn the right to a guaranteed second strike by making a substantial contribution in both money and men to the joint nuclear defence of the partnership. The durability of these arrangements would be made plain in a treaty valid for, say, fifty years or until it had been superseded by a world disarmament agreement.

However, until Britain or France, by adopting a federalist policy, makes such a Defence Community possible, a partnership in this form remains out of reach. But the way towards it can be prepared by greater co-operation between the European nations in conventional defence and by the establishment of a multilateral force to which European nations would contribute in return for a share in the formation of nuclear policy, but without securing for Europe the right to reply to a nuclear attack to which the nuclear forces of the alliance did not, for some reason, respond.

In economics, chapter 8 suggested that the Economic Community could not by itself solve Europe's economic problems, many of which have to be dealt with at a wider level. Partnership with America is needed in relation to two major objectives in particular: the stable growth of the Western economy and the effective support of the West for the development of the emergent nations.

After eighteen years of postwar boom the economy of the free world is developing too many weaknesses. Unless the bold experiment of the Common Market is followed by a substantial cut in tariffs on trade between the European Community and the rest of the world, the general postwar trend towards lower tariffs and greater international trade is likely to be reversed. This sea change would come on top of two serious existing defects: first, an apparently secular stagnation of commodity markets that has for years now been a drag on the exports and hence the effective demand of the developing countries of Asia, Africa and Latin America as well as of the agricultural exporters of temperate zones; secondly, a shortage of international liquidity that keeps the brake more or less permanently on the expansion of the bulk of the industrialised economies of the West. If, in these circumstances, there is a tendency towards autarchy and conflict among the Western nations, it will be impossible not only to ensure their steady economic growth but also to safeguard against stagnation or even a disastrous collapse. Indeed, it is not enough just to avoid conflict or lack of co-operation: a strengthening of the framework of organisation of the free world economy, now skeletally represented by the GATT—IMF—World Bank trinity, is urgently required; and this is one of the main tasks for Atlantic partnership.

The first reaction of the American government to the prospect of an enlarged Common Market was the Trade Expansion Act. If, despite de Gaulle, the consequent negotiations in GATT succeed, the problem of keeping open the channels of trade in the manufacture of the industrialised West will have been solved for some years to come; for there will be regular reductions of tariffs on a very wide front. The United States and other agricultural exporters are insisting at the same time on better terms for agricultural produce as well as for manufactures. The negotiations on industrial products may come to grief over a refusal by the European Community to meet this just demand; or the Community may offer enough concessions in agriculture to enable the negotiations to succeed. But the intractable problems of agricultural trade are not likely to be satisfactorily resolved without commodity agreements such as were agreed in principle by Britain and the Six before the veto. As has been explained, Britain, the main importer of foodstuffs, can hardly, while she is weakened by exclusion from the Economic Community, be expected to agree to pay higher prices for her imports of foodstuffs from temperate producers, although she could contribute to a scheme for the distribution of food to developing countries. Yet, while the incomes of exporters could not at present be much increased by world agreements, they could be stabilised, and the framework for world trade would be correspondingly strengthened.

As well as increasing the vigour and stability of world trade, better conditions for international trade in manufactures and agricultural produce would improve the position of those advanced countries that remain outside the great trading blocs, in particular the countries of the Commonwealth (Australia, Canada and New Zealand) and of EFTA, and Japan.

It has been shown that, although de Gaulle can hamper the working of the Economic Community in many ways and can continue to veto the entry of new members indefinitely, he cannot prevent the Five from cutting tariffs after 1965 if they are determined to do so; for from the end of that year the Community's commercial policy, including the level of its external tariff, becomes subject to majority vote. The same applies to agricultural policies, although here the gaullists might find the sabotaging of commodity agreements too big a price to pay for the pleasure of disrupting Atlantic co-operation. Thus even if France is ruled by de Gaulle or a gaullist after 1965, the Atlantic partnership can nevertheless be realised in the field of trade, so long as the Five have the cohesion to form a policy and the necessary courage to use their voting power.

If shortage of money is not to inhibit economic growth and endanger stability, it is necessary that more international liquidity should be provided, and that the burden now falling on the two key currencies, sterling and the dollar, should be more evenly spread over the currencies of other Western countries, and particularly those of the European Community. There are several ways in which this can be done, on which the French government would not be able to cast a veto.

An increase of liquidity, though necessary, would in itself be a mere stop-gap, and in the longer run a more radical reconstruction of the world monetary system is required. The most imaginative scheme is that put forward by Professor Triffin, whereby the International Monetary Fund would be given some of the attributes of a world central bank in the creation and control of credit. It is to be doubted whether Keynesian policies can ensure stable economic growth at world, and consequently at national, level unless a powerful credit instrument of this sort is devised. But to create it is a political act, implying some control over national monetary and financial policies: a breach in the citadel of economic sovereignty. This is not possible unless a form of political control of the Community type is devised at the same time.

It cannot be envisaged that such political control would be established in any strength as between the United States and the separate European nations, for this would be the economic hegemony that nobody wants. Nor, for reasons explained above, can an Atlantic Community be envisaged, at least for the time being. Here as elsewhere, partnership is the proper form of collaboration, with the American and European partners co-ordinating their international credit policies. Within this framework, and indeed before a united partner has evolved in Europe, there is room for some progress in the direction of a more organised international credit system by means, as Triffin has suggested, of giving the IMF the power to dispose of a limited increment of credit each year.

The Western nations at present make some attempt to co-ordinate their economic policies within the OECD. It should be possible to elaborate stronger methods of co-ordination between Atlantic partners; it is desirable to do so in order to improve the effectiveness of policies and planning in providing the international conditions for economic growth; and it will be essential to do so if at some time in the future the hands of both partners are to be on the lever of credit creation, which activates the operation of economic policies as a whole.

The prosperity of the West is itself a great help to the emergent nations for, by strengthening the demand for their products, it gives an impulse to their growth and provides them with the means to buy their resulting requirements of capital goods. But one of the chief objects of an Atlantic partnership should be to bind itself to long-term policies that will be as helpful as possible to the development of the emergent nations. This is such a central part of the process of creating a world order that the whole of the next chapter is devoted to it. As with the formation of trade and monetary policies to steer the economy of the West, common trade policies towards the developing countries cannot be vetoed after 1965 if the Five will use their majority vote, and aid policies can be developed without France if de Gaulle will not co-operate and the others are prepared to proceed without him.

Thus, although the consolidation of Monnet's Europe will be obstructed by de Gaulle, a form of partnership is possible in the economic field, based on the Economic Community's majority vote for external commercial policies and agriculture, and the ability of the members to act independently if necessary in the spheres of economic and monetary policy. However, until France again supports the Community method, it will be a halting type of partnership, lamed by the difficulty of forming liberal policies for the Community in the teeth of French opposition; unless, that is to say, de Gaulle were to walk out of the Community and France be succeeded by a genuinely Community-minded Britain. In defence no partnership can be had until Britain or France is federalist enough to

accept a European Defence Community; until then the most
that can be expected is a preparation for partnership through
greater co-operation between European nations in the conventional field and the creation of a multilateral nuclear
force under American leadership. The period of struggle with
de Gaulle, then, need not be wasted time; if the Five act with
conviction, if the British choose clearly in favour of the Community method, and if the Americans hold fast to their en-
lightened Atlantic policies, this period can be a useful prelude
to partnership.

The needs of those advanced nations outside the Soviet
bloc that are not at present part of the two main pillars of
partnership—the United States and the European Community—could be catered for in a variety of ways. Membership
of the Community should be open to those European countries that wish to join, and association made possible for others
that apply for it on reasonable terms. There seems to be no
valid reason why either status should not be open in the long
run to Australia, Canada or New Zealand if they want it;
they are after all European countries in all but the geographi-
cal sense, which modern transport renders less and less important. The relationship with Japan should be one of growing
partnership. All these nations should be members of the
OECD for the co-ordination of their economic policies; most
of them are members of NATO for their collective defence. In
this way they would become an integral part of the Atlantic
partnership, gathered around its two main pillars.

The attitude of the partnership towards the emergent
nations is considered in detail in the next chapter; that towards Russia in the following one. Here, however, it is worth
repeating that the political purpose of the partnership is to
work for the "more orderly world that we must have if we
are to escape destruction", not by attempting to dominate the
world but by helping to apply to its affairs the principles of
partnership and Community.

This being so, the partners should make their principles
quite clear from the start. There is a severe danger that any
formal collaboration between them would be construed by
other nations as an effort to use their immense power to
establish a world hegemony. There is indeed the obvious
possibility that, feeling this power in their hands, they would
in fact acquire the habits of domination. The Atlantic nations

should therefore as soon as possible, during the period of prelude to partnership, announce their intention to subscribe to a program of unprecedented scope for the development of Asia, Africa and Latin America : the New Deal for the emergent that is outlined in the next chapter. The emergent nations are rightly becoming increasingly restive at the stagnation of their trade with the West and the failure of Western nations to do much about it. If the only act of partnership has been to initiate negotiations in GATT designed to reduce tariffs for the benefit of the advanced industrialised countries, the anger of the emergent is liable to boil over at the World Trade Conference in mid-1964, and the organisation of the world economy, and eventually of world politics, could move in a direction that was acutely unpleasant for the West. So it is urgent that, despite their preoccupation with the consequences of de Gaulle, the prospective members of the Atlantic partnership should proclaim the launching of a New Deal of massive scope, which, by the very fact that it was designed to increase the strength of the emergent nations many times over, would show that the West is not intent upon domination.

It is therefore to a consideration of the scope and form of a New Deal such as this that we now turn our attention.

12

A NEW DEAL FOR THE EMERGENT NATIONS

A New Deal for the emergent nations necessary for world order; European living standards in a generation

THE Bomb has burned deep into the consciousness of the Western world. Its mushroom cloud is the recurrent nightmare of our generation. Yet for two-thirds of mankind in Asia, Africa and Latin America it is a distant, shadowy thing : for the people, reality is poverty; for those responsible for economic development, danger is the prospect that population may outstrip supplies of food.

The condition of mankind's underdeveloped majority is not only scandalous in itself; it is one of the world's great sources of potential disorder and a peril to the advanced societies of Europe and America. There will clearly be a political explosion if the population explosion leads to mass famine. If famine is avoided but hopes of rising above the level of grinding poverty are repeatedly disappointed, governments will turn to foreign adventures to distract attention from the peoples' grievances and will employ increasingly brutal, dictatorial methods at home. The only alternative to this balkanised chaos, with the constant danger that a world war will be ignited, is rapid and regular economic growth.

If the economies are to develop fast enough, vast resources for investment and for the education and training of the people are required. Resources on this scale cannot be squeezed out of the bare living of the people unless a totalitarian discipline is imposed. So rapid growth requires either help on a large scale from the wealthier nations, or the establishment of powerful dictatorships, whether communist and a strategic menace to the West or nationalist and probably a threat to their neighbours.

It is clearly in the interest of the wealthy West to provide this help. This will not only enable growth to be quicker than if the developing countries have to pull themselves up by their own bootstraps; it will also allow these countries to grow fast without resorting to totalitarian methods. As well as being bad in themselves, such methods engender aggressive leviathans, in contrast to the pacific inclinations of more plural societies. The evolution of democracy based on the plural society is the great political achievement of the West, and there should be no false shame about encouraging the development of such societies, with their bias against war and in favour of welfare, in other parts of the world. Help in taking some of the harshness out of the process of economic growth is one of the best contributions that can be made to this end.

This consideration becomes still more important if it is understood that the Community method must one day be employed at world level, in order to deal with problems of security and world trade. This is the logical end of Monnet's revolution, without which it is not possible to envisage a satisfactory world order. But a world-wide Community would not work if any substantial proportion of its members were totalitarian dictatorships. De Gaulle's regime is far from totalitarian but it is authoritarian enough to have already shown how incompatible are the two concepts of international Community and of dictatorship. Thus it is in the West's interest, and indeed in that of mankind as a whole, that economic growth should be as painless as is possible, in order both to maintain peace and security in the coming years and to lay the foundations of an eventual world order within a democratic world Community.

Although the political reasons for a helpful policy towards the emergent nations are paramount, there are valid economic considerations as well. In economies that were impeccably managed along Keynesian lines, there would be no need of outside stimuli to demand. But unfortunately the management of Western economies is far from perfect, and stronger demand from the emergent nations would be of considerable benefit to the West, now that the postwar boom has slackened away. It is also desirable to safeguard supplies of raw materials and foodstuffs by having friendly relations with the suppliers. And, looking far ahead, a prosperous and open world market will eventually be necessary if full advantage is to be taken of the scope for specialisation and mass production that is continually being enlarged by the advance of science and technology.

The West should therefore, for its security and prosperity, help to build up the economic strength of the emergent nations. This process is not without risk. Gratitude does not fall within the gamut of political emotions, and such strength might be turned against the West. This risk is surely less than that of leaving the emergent either to stagnate or to fall prey to totalitarian regimes; but the choice to build up their strength is likely to be based less on a rational assessment of the relative risks than on a belief that it is the right thing to do. The real answer to the question "why?" is "because".

Western nations do, of course, have multifarious policies and institutions to help the emergent. But the results are too meagre because the effort is ill-organised and the resources inadequate. If Europe and America have the wisdom to give this problem the weight it deserves, they will need to put far more of their political energies into solving it. It was noted at the end of the last chapter that the West would do well to anticipate the World Trade Conference in 1964 with positive proposals for the better organisation of the world economy; and that moves towards Atlantic partnership should, consonant with the idea's liberal and open nature, be synchronised with such proposals. It follows that the first phase of Monnet's revolution, the striving towards Atlantic partnership, should be accompanied by a start to the second phase, in the form of a great drive to quicken the economic growth of developing countries: Europe and America together launching a New Deal for the emergent.

Perhaps a hundred nations throughout the world would participate in such a venture. It is essential that they should understand what is being done and why. The main purpose of a New Deal would be to build up the economies of the emergent so that they can live side by side with the industrialised nations without inferiority; so that peaceful relations between the two groups will be fostered; and so that they will eventually establish together a world Community that could be a solid foundation for peace and security.

The most effective way of showing what is to be done would be to explain what can be achieved in the lifetime of those who are young today. This, the economic objective of the New Deal, could be the achievement throughout the major regions of the developing world of living standards such as those at present normal in Europe.

Progress at this rate is perfectly feasible. Most of the plans of developing countries envisage economic growth of five to seven per cent a year compound or even more, and growth at five per cent a year is not uncommonly being achieved. At a later stage of development, Japan and Russia have shown that still faster rates of even eight to ten per cent a year compound are possible. With the full support of advanced nations, it should certainly be possible to maintain growth at five to seven per cent a year; and even those countries such as India, where grinding poverty prevails and the average income is some ten shillings a week, and where population is increasing rapidly, could at these rates be raised up to current European levels during the lifetime of those who are now children.

Progress in developing countries depends, of course, more than anything on their own efforts. But those efforts will be made more confidently if the necessary external support is assured. Europe and America should therefore study what is likely to be required in order to achieve such rates of growth, and then declare themselves ready to play their full part by providing both aid, technical and educational as well as financial, and better conditions for the exports of the emergent.

Planning for trade and aid; a world initiative by the Atlantic partnership

If the New Deal is to be effective, it must comprise a comprehensive policy for trade and aid. "Trade not aid" is a foolish slogan; the emergent countries get about a quarter of their foreign exchange from imports of capital and grants, and any sharp cut in the amount would inhibit economic growth. Earnings from exports are, nevertheless, the more important and they do not mortgage the future by piling up an annual burden of interest payments and an eventual obligation to pay in full. Thus the first task of the New Deal should be to improve the markets for the emergent countries' exports.

The most valuable contribution to this would be steady economic growth in both Europe and America, the conditions for which were considered in chapter 11. For some primary products, commodity agreements would be desirable in order to iron out wild fluctuations in export earnings, and there is much scope for improving access to the markets of advanced countries by cutting tariffs and internal taxes.

During the Brussels negotiations, Britain and the Six agreed in principle on certain tariff cuts on tropical products, on some world-wide commodity agreements, on association for Commonwealth countries in Africa and on comprehensive trade agreements for those in Asia. These techniques could have their part in a New Deal for the emergent and they could be put into effect without waiting for Britain to join the Economic Community, just as the suspension of the Community tariffs on tea and tropical hardwoods and the offer of association to Commonwealth countries in Africa have already been made. But it would be important, in the course of a New Deal, to take the sting out of association by gradually removing all tariffs on imports of tropical produce into Europe and America; in this way the preferences given by the Community and by Britain, which are a thorn in the flesh of nations outside the preferential areas, would disappear.

Some countries are rich enough in tropical products or minerals to earn from exports all the foreign exchange they need. Others, and in particular India and Pakistan, have scant prospect of raising their earnings unless they can increase their exports of manufactures. Quite apart from the political need to support these countries' economies, it is in the interest of high-wage countries to take advantage of the international division of labour by exchanging their capital-intensive products for the labour-intensive manufactures of countries such as India. Import quotas or high tariffs on such manufactures should therefore be regarded as no more than a stop-gap, with a time-table for the elimination of the quotas and the reduction of the tariffs to a moderate or low level. At the same time an international fund should be instituted, analogous to the Social Fund of the Economic Community, a somewhat similar American scheme associated with the Trade Expansion Act, or the British arrangements for buying out surplus capacity in the cotton industry, with the object of accelerating the reduction of capacity in labour-intensive industries in the advanced countries, which at present tend to hang tenaciously on to these millstones.

Like the proposed programme of tariff cuts following the Trade Expansion Act, the cuts in tariffs on the products of emergent countries and the relaxation of quota restrictions could be undertaken according to a regular agreed schedule over a period of years; and, as we have emphasised, the Economic Community could make such cuts by majority vote after the end of 1965, thus enabling partnership to function in relation to the New Deal, so long as the Five are determined that it will. Commodity agreements and financial or educational aid can likewise not be thwarted by the veto.

Economic aid often evokes an image of vast numbers of dollars being poured either into steel mills in the middle of the desert, producing steel of high cost and low quality for which there is no market, or else into the pockets of the cousins and nephews of a corrupt ruler of some small but supposedly anti-communist state. Of course this image is a distorted one. The great proportion of money going to a country such as India is used effectively for sensible and indeed essential purposes, and the need is for twice as much of this sort of aid not for less of it. But it is nevertheless true that money cannot be properly used for economic development by those who lack the will or the skill to use it; and aid for education and training as well as technical assistance is therefore of primary importance.

As the emergent countries have too few people of their own with technical qualifications, they have to borrow such people from abroad and particularly from Europe and America. But technical assistance of this sort should be regarded as a temporary expedient. The aim should be to enable the developing countries to do all the necessary jobs with their own people, and for this a vast programme of training and education is required.

Despite books, wireless, television and films, there is no real substitute for teachers meeting students face to face in order to transmit knowledge, ways of thinking and attitudes to work; hence the flow of teachers from the advanced countries to the developing ones and of students in the opposite direction. Britain and France have made the biggest effort in relation to their resources, with large numbers of overseas students at their universities, technical colleges and teachers' training colleges as well as getting practical training in factories, hospitals and other places of work, and many British and French people teaching in the emergent countries. The other European countries and the United States, and increasingly the Russians, also make a growing contribution. Britain at present devotes not far from ten per cent of its total higher educational facilities to students from overseas, and ten per cent might be a suitable target for the advanced countries as a whole. For economy, the effort should be concentrated towards the higher end of the educational scale; and for reasons of language, national psychology and efficiency as well, it should concentrate on the teaching of those who will teach and train others when they go home. This policy of investment in teachers increases the gap to be filled by technical assistance at first but it holds out the prospect of closing it later on.

Educational help and technical assistance are the primary need of developing countries; but however healthy their exports, they will need large amounts of financial aid if growth rates of five to seven per cent are indeed to be achieved.

Two aspects of the present effort may be criticised : the quantity and the organisation. During the four years of the Marshall Plan, the United States supplied an average of four billion dollars a year to Europe whereas the West as a whole provided six billion dollars in grants and official loans for the emergent nations in 1961. Europe and America taken together are now twice as rich as the United States was at the time of the Marshall Plan; and each dollar is worth less because of inflation. Thus the total effort for the emergent nations is, despite rapid expansion in recent years, still relatively less than that made by the Americans through the Marshall Plan after the war. In the past it could rightly be reasoned that there was a shortage of sound projects in the developing countries rather than a shortage of money. But this is no longer true. Economic progress in India would be accelerated if the import requirements under the Indian Plan could be met; although the quantity of aid is considerable, the plan has to be cut back because it is not big enough. Nor is Nigeria within sight of finding the external resources needed to finance its not very ambitious plan.

If the quantity of the aid effort is too small, its organisation is also deficient. A plethora of national and international organisations has sprung up since the war to meet specific needs, and it is time that some order and coherence were imposed.

Marshall Aid, as a great act of creative statesmanship, generated innovations that are a model for those who later encounter similar problems. One of its most remarkable features was the demand by doctrinaire capitalist America that Europe should draw up long-term plans for the use of the aid. After estimating requirements and deciding on the approximate size of their offer, the Americans promised their aid for a period of four years and the European governments were asked, as a condition of receiving it, to draw up four-year plans showing their likely economic growth and consequent import requirements.

A similar procedure could be applied to the New Deal: an offer by the advanced countries, based on their estimates of requirements if the desirable growth of trade and aid is to be achieved; followed by a detailed general plan based on the national plans of the emergent nations. This general plan could aim at the necessary growth of trade by general tariff reductions arranged in GATT and through comprehensive trade agreements with individual countries, as well as the stabilisation of trade through world commodity agreements. Existing institutions could likewise be used for the programme of aid, provided that their efforts were properly co-ordinated. Regional development banks or funds such as the Inter-American Development Bank or the Colombo Plan, which are repositories of knowledge about their regions, would be powerful instruments of co-ordination.

If the advanced and the emergent nations were of similar strength, there would be a clear case for their joining together in Community-type institutions to organise the New Deal. But the emergent would justifiably fear that such a Community would be merely an institutionalised hegemony, a new form of empire; for the advanced nations, if they acted in concert, would be predominantly strong. Until the emergent have greatly increased their strength and confidence, therefore, the New Deal would have to be organised mainly within inter-governmental rather than supranational bodies, though there is doubtless some scope for supranational features in the arrangements for world commodity agreements, for example.

The regional Economic Commissions of the United Nations seem to be the best bodies for the purpose. Within their regions they enjoy almost universal membership, approval and support. The Economic Commissions for Africa and for Latin America cover suitable regions for the purpose; the Economic Commission for Asia and the Far East would probably best be split into one Commission for South Asia and one for South East Asia. A Commission for the Middle East, so far impeded by the dispute between Arabs and Jews, would have to be set up; and if China were to take part, it would be a region on its own. Thus the emergent countries would form five or six regions for the planning of the New Deal.

It is to be hoped that all the advanced nations would participate, with the initiative coming from those that want to establish the Atlantic partnership. Having decided on the scope of the effort they want to make, the OECD members could sound out the Russians to discover whether they would contribute on a similar scale. Whatever the answer, the offer would be made to the emergent just as General Marshall made his offer to Europe in 1947. There could not be a better occasion than the World Trade Conference that is due to take place seventeen years later.

If this New Deal were to get under way, the spectre of starvation would be banished; the danger of war from political instability in the emergent nations would decline; and the organisation of the world economy would be improved, reducing the danger of violent slumps or prolonged stagnation. Moreover, the foundations of a partnership between the advanced and the emergent would be laid. For the strength of the emergent would be increased so that they would be less fearful of domination; and the programme of education and technical aid, with large numbers of students, teachers and technically qualified people moving from one part of the world to the other, would in fact be a vast exercise in cultural exchange. Such a partnership is one of the pre-conditions of an eventual world Community.

It is not likely that de Gaulle would agree to support a programme such as this. Not that he would have any mean objection to the peoples of the emergent nations getting more to eat. Nor would he, however, have a positive enough desire that they do so to enable him to swallow his dislike of a project in which the Americans and probably also the United Nations were involved; nor would any understanding of the political needs of the times enable him to overcome a propensity to channel all France's favours, and if possible those of France's Common Market partners, to the three per cent or so of the population of the underdeveloped world who live in African countries formerly ruled by France.

The New Deal would, on the other hand, be a natural policy for the supporters of Monnet's Europe. It would spread the liberal methods of international democracy across the world. In Europe it would be the perfect backbone for a common European foreign policy : a vital issue in which the interests of European countries largely coincide; amenable to the detailed programmes and timetable techniques of the Community, because concerned with measurable quantities; and suitable for the taking of decisions by majority vote.

The decisions of commercial policy required for the New Deal can, as has already been pointed out, be taken by majority vote in the Community after 1965, and those concerning aid and education cannot at any time be vetoed by France. Thus, if the Five are determined they can, with Britain and America and any other advanced nations that wish to do so, take part in launching the programme without the help and even against the opposition of de Gaulle. But it is hard enough for democracies to decide on bold action with the use of large resources until it is too late; with the thorn of de Gaulle in the flesh of the Five, movement is rendered still more difficult. The prospects for a full-blooded programme will therefore be much better when the battle against gaullism has been won. Meanwhile, a project as liberal and as constructive of world order as a New Deal for the emergent provides a perfect field for encounter between the Europeans and de Gaulle.

13

TOWARDS WORLD ORDER

**Towards disarmament and world Community; Atlantic partnership
and the New Deal ideological reassessment; partnership with Russia**

PROSPERITY for the emergent nations is one foundation of the
more orderly world that Monnet foresees. But a satisfactory
world order will never be created unless the vast destructive
force of modern arms is brought under control. For this the
West and Russia must come to terms.

Monnet believes that this will happen when the West is
irrevocably united. "When the partnership of America and a
United Europe makes it plain to all that the West may
change from within but that others cannot change it by
outside pressures, then Mr. Khrushchev or his successor will
accept the facts, and the conditions will at last exist for turning so-called peaceful coexistence into genuine peace. Then at
last real disarmament will become possible."[1]

A united West undermines the Marxist dogma of conflict
within the capitalist camp and so discourages a hard line in
Moscow. It should therefore make limited agreement more
possible, for example on the test ban that will help to prevent
the spread of nuclear arms. But "real disarmament" requires
a settling of what Monnet calls "philosophic conflicts" based
on "a change in the view which people take of the future";[2]
and it is doubtful whether this will take place until the dogma
of imperialist exploitation has also been disproved. For the
Russians, with Cuba as evidence, will continue to hope that
the emergent nations will pave the way to world communism
by falling into the communist camp, until it is shown that
they are peacefully achieving their economic development
outside it. Thus the success of a New Deal for the emergent
is probably, like a united West, a pre-condition for a change
in the Russian view of the future radical enough to bring
agreement on "real disarmament".

[1] Jean Monnet, "A Ferment of Change", *Journal of Common Market
Studies,* Vol. I, No. 3, p. 210.   [2] *Ibid.*

The meaning of "real disarmament" has become clear during the protracted disarmament negotiations between Russia and the West. Although in practice no progress has been made, in principle both sides agree that the aim is a complete and universal disarmament of national forces down to the levels required for internal security, and the creation of a world force that would be responsible for law and order. After what must have been the most thorough investigation by defence ministries, nobody at the negotiations could deny that this was the only way to bring the forces of mass destruction under control. But, just as the Economic Community is beginning to transfer the seat of power over economic affairs from separate national governments to the European institutions at Brussels, and just as a Defence Community would definitively transfer the physical basis of power to similar European institutions, so a universal disarmament would transfer power into the hands of the institutions controlling the world force.

In Europe, at least until the advent of de Gaulle, it has been possible to convince those who feel their interests to be identified with national systems of government, who naturally include most of those people who carry political power, that the Community method would add to their influence, not detract from it. For the main decisions are taken by the national governments acting together in the Council of Ministers. The voting system and the relations between the different parts of the Community institutions are designed so that no one nation is likely to be repeatedly in a minority. The national governments therefore expect to have the power of the Community instead of just their own nation behind decisions with most of which they are likely to agree; and, where they are in an outvoted minority, they are not likely to find the decisions too distasteful because they have confidence in the broad identity of the attitudes and interests of themselves and their partners.

As between Russia and the West, however, the situation is quite different. Although there is complete identity of interest in the avoidance of nuclear war, attitudes and interests on most other questions diverge sharply. A Community system of control for a world force would, if decisions by majority were, as in the Economic Community, hard to get, be usually in a state of indecision. In a new venture such as a world force, it

would in any case be a problem to ensure the establishment of
political control over the military. If the political machinery
broke down, the military, or that sector of the world force
that came out on top, would almost certainly take the law
into its own hands. If, on the other hand, the Community
voting system were strong enough for clear decisions to be
taken, the Russians would surely reason that they would be
outvoted by the world's non-communist majority. The last
generation of Soviet leaders would have believed that this
would result in their being personally liquidated by the
capitalists; the present ones would almost certainly fear that
their political power and the form of society in which they
believe would be dismantled.

If, on the other hand, the communists make further en-
croachments in the emergent regions of the world, to the
extent that they would feel safe in transferring the physical
basis of power to the institutions of a world Community in
which the political balance was held by the emergent nations,
then the Western governments would be unwilling to transfer
power to it for fear that the plural societies of the West would
be destroyed and the Western political class treated like the
democratic politicians of Eastern Europe.

In short, real disarmament, which implies a world Community, is not at present possible, not because governments
are stupid or obstinate, but because there is not the mutual
trust that such a Community would demand between its main
political and regional groups: the communists, the emergent
and the West. For the time being, the universal disarmament
and the world force that both the Russians and the West
agree to be essential in principle are impossible in practice,
and attempts to stabilise the co-existence of super-powers,
each possessing the means to destroy civilisation and perhaps
to exterminate mankind, are the best that can be expected.

But this precarious balance of terror is profoundly unsatisfactory. No reasonable person can rest content until the nightmare of extermination has been removed. And this cannot be
done without mutual trust between the Russians and the
West: that is, without a settlement of their "philosophic
conflicts".

People in the West, and probably in Russia too, are becoming increasingly aware that such a settlement is possible. The
militant intransigence of the communists has been based on

false dogmas about the nature of the West: the inability of the nineteenth century capitalist system to remedy its own defects, including a supposedly iron law that the poor would get poorer while the rich got richer; the inevitability of war between the capitalist powers; the certainty of imperialist exploitation. The analysis on which these dogmas were based enriched political thinking at the time of their origin; their perpetuation through the 'thirties was, to say the least, understandable; in the early years after the war the old generation of Bolsheviks, nurtured in hatred and violence, were not likely to abandon them. But since the war the Keynesian reform of capitalism has had remarkable success; apart from chauvinism's gaullist death pangs, the "imperialists" have been moving fast to a federation in Europe and an Atlantic partnership; the old empires have been dismantled. Already in the light of these facts and of the aweful dangers of the hydrogen bomb, the Russian communists have overthrown the dogma of the inevitability of war, although facts and danger alike seem of little interest to the Chinese. Given a stronger organisation of the Western economy through an Atlantic partnership and a definitive repulse of gaullism by the federalists and Europeans, the successful reform of the capitalist economic system as well as the peaceful relations between Western nations will become plain to all but the blind; and the doctrine of neo-colonialism, which is the new look for imperialist exploitation, would be eroded by a New Deal that built up the economies of the emergent so as to make them less dependent on the West. There is therefore every reason to suppose that, if Monnet's revolution is pursued by means of Atlantic partnership and a New Deal for the emergent, the communists of Russia and Eastern Europe will continue their ideological reassessment until it has become a radical transformation.

The West for its part is not only in the process of disproving fundamental Marxist dogmas; it is also meeting some of the juster criticisms of the communists. To the welfare states of the West are being added techniques of flexible economic planning; not only is the possibility of war between the capitalists obsolescent, but Community and the prospect of partnership have blunted the edge of greedy and competing nationalisms in all but the gaullists; and America is in the throes of a great movement towards racial justice. In the West, too, it is being increasingly realised, as the late Pope

John's "Peace on Earth" Encyclical showed, that the communists of Russia and Eastern Europe are not devils incarnate
but men wrestling with the problems of government that inevitably arise from the tensions between human nature and
modern technology. Since human nature and modern technology are much the same in Russia and in the West, it
should be possible eventually to settle "philosophic conflicts"
by reaching some consensus as to the principles by which
such problems are to be solved.

But this process cannot be left to chance. So long as the
balance of terror remains, civilisation hangs by a thread. A
positive effort is therefore required to overcome the centrifugal forces of national cultures reinforced by opposing ideolo-
gies. With Atlantic partnership secured and a New Deal for
the emergent launched, it will be necessary to lay the foundations for partnership with Russia.

As within the West, such partnership will be created by
practical co-operation and cultural exchange. It will take
longer and a big effort will be needed, because the initial gap
is desperately wide. But meetings with Russians such as the
Pugwash conferences should be encouraged and multiplied;
advantage should be taken of the greater opportunities for
contact with people in Poland, Hungary, Rumania and Yugo-
slavia; and the ground be thus prepared for a much vaster
programme of exchanges to take place as the ideological
climate improves, consequent upon the success of Atlantic
partnership and the New Deal. The thought of Western
partnership with the Russians may be startling at first, but if
Monnet's revolution proceeds it will come more and more to
seem a natural development.

Thus the road from Monnet's Europe to a world order has
three stages. The first stage is the evolution of an Atlantic
partnership in which Europe and America bind themselves to
carry through long-term policies for the better organisation of
the world economy and for speeding the development of the
emergent nations. This partnership would also consolidate the
defence co-operation between both sides of the Atlantic, thus
reducing the risk of a resurgence of Soviet militancy caused
by a split in the Western alliance.

The second stage would be the New Deal for the emergent,
in which the Atlantic partners, including Japan and other
members of OECD and, it is to be hoped, together with the

Russians, would make a major political and economic effort to help the emergent nations to quicken their economic development. This would render the politics of the developing regions more stable and thus reduce the danger of war; enable the emergent nations more easily to evolve democratic, plural and hence pacific societies; build up their economic strength until they should have no fear of consorting with the advanced nations in a world Community; and develop a form of planning for trade and aid in the United Nations regional Economic Commissions that would be a springboard for later moves towards the Community method. The New Deal would in fact be a vast and sustained effort to create a partnership between the advanced and the emergent nations, based on three main elements: practical co-operation in the planning of trade and aid; cultural exchanges in the massive movement of people for the programmes of education and technical assistance; and the growth of a balance of strength on which partnership and later Community can be based.

The third stage on the road towards world order would be the drive for a partnership with Russia on which real disarmament could be based.

These three stages would overlap. Thus it has already been suggested that the first act of an Atlantic partnership should be to launch a New Deal for the emergent. Moreover, whereas the Russians would probably not be amenable to ideas of partnership with the West until the New Deal was well under way and the continued development of the emergent nations outside the Soviet bloc therefore assured, the process of creating a partnership with Russia, once started, might not take very long. Thus the Russians and the West might be able to conclude a thorough-going agreement on disarmament long before the emergent nations had developed their strength to the point where they would be ready to throw in their lot with the advanced nations in a supranational world Community.

A further uncertainty in the timing of progress towards world order is China. It is impossible to guess when the great wall of incomprehension that now separates China from almost all the rest of the world will be broken down. Perhaps the Chinese will leave their fanaticism behind them in a very few decades; perhaps they will remain for a long time as the last outpost of chauvinism, while all the rest of the world has become ready to establish a world Community. In either case, other peoples should make what progress they can, endeavouring the while to bring China into the family of nations, and allowing her to participate in world institutions if she agrees to do so.

One cannot be precise now about the political form of the world order that would eventually emerge. But, since the problem of composing the wills of nation-states is essentially similar to that which has confronted the Europeans, it may be supposed that there would be similarities in the solution. The national governments, acting together, would doubtless play the main part in arriving at decisions. If the world Community took the form of a strengthened United Nations, the Security Council, representing the great powers and the main regions of the world and gradually abandoning the veto, could be the Council of Ministers for disarmament and world security, while the Economic and Social Council could be the Council of Ministers for international trade and monetary problems. The General Assembly, perhaps reformed on a more representative basis, could be analogous to the Community's Parliament; the UN Secretariat to its independent executive; and the International Court of Justice to its Court. The voting system would reflect a balance between the main political forces in the world, at present the West, the Soviet bloc and the emergent nations.

Monnet's revolution: a new theory and practice of foreign policy

The vision of a world Community is the logical end of Monnet's revolution, contrasting with the gaullist harking back to 1913 when the world was dominated by an uneasy combination of half-a-dozen European powers. De Gaulle's ambitions are probably impractical and, as the year 1914 vividly illustrates, certainly undesirable. It would be idle to suggest that the working out of Monnet's revolution will be an easy process; on the contrary, it will be hard and long. But while the full vision, if splendid, is a distant one, the process lends itself to practical progress step by step.

This progress requires the radical reversal of the traditional objectives and methods of foreign policy. The aim can no longer be the imperialist one of national aggrandisement and its logical consequence, world domination. Nor is the League of Nations' dream of a hundred good little nations coexisting

without coercion any more than a ludicrous fantasy of doctrinaire liberalism. The objective now must be to solve the
nations' common problems by building for them common
institutions. For not only is this morally better than domination; it is also in the present age more practical. Democracies
are bad at domination; the opposite principle that permeates
their national politics has the habit of spilling over into their
conduct of foreign policy. Even if the modern West had any
stomach for imperialism, it could not satisfy its appetite for
the power of Russia would bar the way. Above all, science
and technology have pressed the nations so close together that
their common interests are now in fact much more important
than their conflicts. Their interest in survival and hence in
control of the Bomb transcends any benefits they might hope
to secure from the competing use of national power. The
world economy is becoming so united that depression any-
where casts a shadow on prosperity everywhere; an economic
policy devoted to grabbing a larger share of the world's cake
is less advantageous, even for the narrow national interest of
the grabber, than a policy designed to make the cake itself
grow as fast as possible.

For no peoples have these considerations more force than
for those of Europe. Crowded into the western tip of Eurasia,
they would get short shrift if the pursuit of national power
were to lead to nuclear war. Their open economies would
suffer grievously were the world economy to break down.
Morally and intellectually, the peoples of Europe can never
be at rest until they have helped to construct a political
framework strong enough to contain the genies of science and
of nationalism that they themselves have, in recent centuries,
uncorked and discharged upon the world.

Thus doctrinaire nationalists, whether devils incarnate such
as Hitler or more traditional power politicians such as de
Gaulle, are a menace to everyone and particularly to the
peoples of Europe. National governments must, of course,
continue to look after their legitimate interests and, so long
as national military power remains, to prevent the balance of
power from tilting against them. But the pursuit of national
interest and power can no longer be the fundamental aim of
policy; as such it must be replaced by the effort to identify
the general interest and to embody it in common institutions
that group the nations together.

It follows from this change of objectives that the tools of foreign policy cannot be just the coalition, the balance of power, the assertion of national grandeur and all the other techniques of Machiavellian diplomacy. Nor is the well-intended internationalist paraphernalia of summit meetings, inter-governmental conferences and non-aggression pacts enough. Many of these techniques must still be used. But diplomacy can no longer be constructive unless it employs the methods that stem from Monnet's revolution. First, the search for common interests and the focusing of attention upon them. Secondly, the creation of partnerships centred on agreement about common interests; cemented by personal understanding deliberately fostered by cultural exchanges; embodied by the partners in long-term agreements to co-operate; based on an equality between the partners that is a function of their real strength not a fiction of international law. Thirdly, the conversion of partnerships into Communities when the balance of national forces, the evolution of plural societies and the growth of mutual trust are far enough developed to make international democracy a workable proposition.

This cumulative process starts naturally with those nations that are geographically, economically and culturally closest to one another. But it must continue until the evolution outlined in this chapter is complete : until partnerships between the main regions of the world have been developed to the point where a world Community can be established. This is the only sane and reasonable prospect for the world : Monnet's revolution in powerful and articulated action.

There will be those who say that the whole conception is utopian : that people who reach for the stars in this way are likely to fall flat on their faces. But this was repeatedly said of the projects for the European Communities; it was said, for that matter, of the federalist proposals of the Founding Fathers of the United States of America. It is liable to be said of any idea that may change the course of history. Whether or not the conception is utopian depends not on whether the intention is to achieve something great or something small, but on whether the style of action proposed is practical or not. And the methods of Monnet's revolution are essentially pragmatic : not a reaching for the stars, but one step after another up the side of a mountain.

It will also be said that the whole idea is too imaginative

and simply too expensive to be practical politics for a democracy: that electorates cannot understand such far-ranging ideas and that they will not pay huge sums for economic aid or conventional defence. It is possible that this is true. If so, democracy is doomed to disappear, whether in a mushroom cloud or trampled underfoot by dictators. For democracy can survive and flourish only if it adapts itself to the conditions of the age, which demand the extension of government over areas wider than the nation-states, which in turn demands a strenuous and costly effort of statesmanship.

But to assume that democracies are necessarily mean and short-sighted is to misconstrue their nature. They are slow to recognise a new problem and to react to it. Many centres of opinion and of power must be alerted and persuaded before decisions can be taken. But if those with the vision to invent and to lead do not sink into lethargy, the many elements of the plural society will eventually be persuaded, and a formidable explosion of energy can then be released. This was demonstrated most strikingly during the Second World War, when the war effort of the democracies was more total than that of totalitarian Germany. So long as the political class in the West retains its vitality, this will be demonstrated again and the liberal, humane and realistic philosophy of Monnet's revolution will in the end prevail throughout the world.

CONCLUSION

14

EUROPE AGAINST DE GAULLE

THIS book's starting point was the clash between the ideas of Monnet and de Gaulle. From there it has ranged over the major political forces and problems not only of Europe but of the world as a whole.

This is no accident. For the clash is not so much between two men as between two opposing principles. It is one of the great conflicts of our time. Not just Monnet against de Gaulle, but Monnet's Europe against the Europe of nation-states; federalism against nationalism; in the last analysis, order against chaos.

For the peoples of Europe, including the British, the conflict nevertheless starts in Europe. If de Gaulle reawakes the wild passions of nationalism on the Continent, it is hard to imagine what dark things the future may hold. If he succeeds merely in causing continued friction between the European nations, one half of the West will be frustrated and impotent. But if the vital forces of Europe are summoned up to repel gaullist nationalism—if Europe is truly against de Gaulle— then a liberal, democratic, pacific Europe will contribute its great strength to the consolidation of the West and the construction of a world order.

There is no time to lose in assembling the forces of Monnet's Europe. Nineteen sixty-five is probably the crucial year. There will then be a presidential election in France and a general election in Germany. The successors to Dr. Adenauer and a new government in Britain will have had time to run themselves in. The strengths and weaknesses of de Gaulle's campaign to conquer political Europe will have been revealed. The Economic Community will be about to enter its third stage, when majority voting is introduced for vital questions.

Thus 1965 may be a European climacteric. If no single year can be selected as such for the world at large, it is nevertheless impossible to justify delay in dealing with world problems. The sands are running out for mankind unless the Bomb and the economic consequences of the population explosion are brought under control.

In these circumstances, those who do not respond are, in both the Greek and the English sense, idiots. There are many worthy people on the Continent who say that politics is a dirty business and not their concern. There are American isolationists who say the same about European politics although they would not dream of saying it about their own. And there are those British who still believe they can remain insulated from events on the Continent. Have these people learnt nothing from the past thirty years?

For British and Continentals alike, there is no valid alternative to Monnet's Europe. Equivocation and half-measures are useless. Rejection not compromise is the treatment for gaullist nationalism. George Washington said, at the outset of the Philadelphia Convention that drew up the Constitution of the United States, when faint-hearted politicians were proposing to water down the Federal plan on the grounds that it would encounter too much opposition from the sovereign states: "It is too probable that no plan we propose will be adopted. Perhaps another dreadful conflict is to be sustained. If, to please the people, we offer what we ourselves do not approve, how can we afterward defend our work? Let us raise a standard to which the wise and honest can repair; the event is in the hands of God."[1] This was the dictation of a bygone age. But the circumstances today are not dissimilar; and the same uncompromising courage is required.

[1] John Fiske, *The Critical Period of American History, 1783–89*, Houghton, Mifflin Co., Boston, 1888, p. 232.